Praise for *Travels*

'As we travel with Bloch on her j
grief after the death of her beloved
honesty and compassion – both for herself and for the others
she meets as she slowly progresses towards a sort of healing'

Nancy Pearl, librarian, and author of *George & Lizzie*
and the Book Lust series

'Emotionally raw, endearingly wry, and sweetly seductive, *Travels with My Grief* is a journey through the mental, physical, and spiritual terra incognita brought on by loss. Witnessing Bloch pass from the dark, monochromatic landscape of her fractured self into the gloriously sensual environment she launches herself into is like watching Dorothy touch down in Oz or Alice step through the looking glass: disorienting, exhilarating, delightful, and dangerous in equal measure. More than the carnival of colour, curiosities, and customs that the author opens herself to, it is the trust in new friendships, the shared experience of violent trauma, the leaps of faith, and finally, the literal and metaphorical walk through fire that draws us in and allows us to see how our own fears, injuries and isolation might be remedied by a larger love of all that is good in the world'

Kim Barnes, Pulitzer finalist and author of *In the Wilderness: Coming of Age in Unknown Country*

'A scrumptious mix of magenta and indigo, curry and cardamom, pungent marigolds and jangling bangles entices us into this vividly remembered sojourn in India, where author Susan Bloch learned to lay aside her grief and embrace life with fervour and firewalking. A savoury, sensual, sparkling memoir you won't forget'

Dori Jones Yang, author of *When the Red Gates Opened: A Memoir of China's Reawakening*

'Heart-wrenching and gorgeous. *Travels with my Grief* documents the transformation from despair and dysfunction after the death of a beloved soulmate to a spirit-lifting journey full of colour, intense drama, new friendship, a foodie's mouth-watering appreciation of Mumbai's "tandoori chicken, vegetable Biryani, garlicky black lentils, cardamom and ginger," and finally, the exhilaration of dancing again. Not to mention the thrill of walking on glass followed by walking on fire. A marvelous, dazzling memoir'

Priscilla Long, author of *Fire and Stone: Where Do We Come From? What Are We? Where Are We Going?*

'Emotive, funny and wonderfully real, this isn't simply a travelogue. This is compelling life experience writ large. Susan writes with honesty and passion not just about her own story, but the people and places that make life so vital. Her captivating story is an inspiration to us all'

Matthew Smith, Exprimez Publishing Consultancy

'It is so vivid, it's like watching a movie. Every emotion, anxiety, joy and memories are so incredibly penned down, it's like travelling with Susan. This story is an inspiration for many who want to make a change but cannot leave their comfort zone. Take the plunge like Sue did'

Heena Munshaw, managing director,
Beacon Holidays, India

'Susan invites us on her journey through grief, as she seeks new beginnings after the loss of her soulmate'

Kay Hutchison, radio producer, podcaster and author

SUSAN BLOCH

TRAVELS WITH MY GRIEF

A PERSONAL JOURNEY OF LOVE, LOSS AND RECOVERY

Red Door

Published by RedDoor

www.reddoorpress.co.uk

ISBN 978-1915194-06-0

A CIP catalogue record for this book is available from the British Library

Cover design: Rose Cooper

Typesetting: Jen Parker, Fuzzy Flamingo
www.fuzzyflamingo.co.uk

Printed in the UK by CPI Group (UK), Croydon

For John

'All the art of living lies in a fine mingling of letting
go and holding on'

Henry Havelock Ellis

Contents

Prologue

39 Cradock Avenue
Rosebank
Johannesburg
1952

Dear Dad and Mum

I'm so miserable. I hate Aunty Lily and all the fuss she makes of me. She even makes me wear my blue cardigan when I'm not cold. Uncle Harry's moustache scratches my face when he kisses me goodnight and I have to go to sleep at eight sharp.

Please come home.

Love

Sue

I was five, maybe six, and had just learned to write. My mother said she was proud of my writing and kept this letter for years. But this didn't make up for all those nights that I cried myself to sleep.

I remember waving goodbye to my parents at Palmietfontein, Johannesburg's main airport. In those days, overseas vacation travel was almost as exceptional as flying into space today. It took three days by propeller plane to get to

Athens via Bulawayo, Nairobi and Khartoum, and six weeks to sail from Southampton to Durban.

Family photographs show a handsome, glamorous couple standing next to a shack, the main terminal. Mum wore a tweed suit, black patent high heels with matching clutch purse and a small pillbox hat with a veil over her forehead. Dad wore his usual, traditional grey suit, and navy-and-grey-striped tie. He smelled of Lifebuoy soap.

Perhaps the clue to my daring personality connects to that adventurous journey my parents took to Europe in the fifties. When they returned, they entertained family and friends for months, and maybe even years, with endless stories and slideshows, over cups of tea and dinner conversations. I listened to tales about gondoliers in blue-and-white-striped shirts singing 'Arrivederci Roma' on the Grand Canal. I could see myself holding hands with Christopher Robin and Alice, at the 'changing of the guard' at Buckingham Palace.

Even today decades later, I still remember the name of the hotel they stayed at in London – The Dorchester near Marble Arch. In the family album, I have photographs of Mum with her sister, Aunty Dolly, a new settler in Tel Aviv, standing on a pile of rubble near what's now the city centre. No wonder as a teen, I fell in love with Charlton Heston in *Exodus*. I inhaled those travel stories – the smell of the beige leather gloves from Rome and the taste of creamy custard of *mille-feuille* on the Champs-Élysées. I swooned at Laurence Olivier's Romeo at the Old Vic, listened to political speeches on soapboxes at Hyde Park and fed the pigeons in Trafalgar Square. I salivated on the first bite of a smoked salmon canapé at the table of the handsome captain on the *Queen Mary*.

I listened to these tales again and again. When I fell asleep, I dreamed of eating fettuccine Alfredo with Parmigiana cheese, smelling lavender in Scotland and watching Margot Fonteyn dancing *Swan Lake* at Sadler's Wells.

When I grow up, I thought, *I'm going to travel and see all those places.*

I did, and so much more.

Did those stories encourage me to smack sixes on our garden cricket pitch and take early Sunday morning bike rides in the open veldt with Peter, the boy next door? Was it then that I first learned to be resilient and adventurous? Maybe that photo of Mum with Aunty Dolly urged me, a young wife and mother living in Tel Aviv decades later, to volunteer to work in a hospital emergency room, and then as a trauma therapist, during the Yom Kippur War?

Family legends shaped me, determined how I became a bona fide international opiates smuggler, when I took my terminally ill husband, John, at his request, to Florida, Paris and Marrakech while he was swallowing morphine to dull the pain. These memories cheered me on when I went back to India after John died. They stopped me from retreating from who I was.

One morning on the way to work in Mumbai, I watched four schoolgirls, from a local slum, giggling and chattering as they walked across a rubbish tip on their way to school. All were identically dressed in ironed blue school uniforms. Buckled satchels on their backs, the red ribbons in their neatly plaited hair bounced along as the girls weaved in between the cars and bikes, their socks a bright white, with polished shoes; shiny and black.

A whiff of ammonia seeped into my air-conditioned car, and exhaust fumes from a nearby bus clouded the window.

For a moment, the girls' image vanished. And then, there they were, laughing and shouting, 'Hello…what's your name?…how old are you?…where you from?'

Rolling down the window and waving back, I realised that like those girls, I needed to meet the world and all its squalor and pain, with intention, pride and gratitude.

And with clean white socks.

LOSS

CHAPTER 1

A Death Bed: February 2005

Snow smothers everything early this winter morning: the church roof in the square across the street, rows of Cyprus trees protecting the cemetery, rubbish bins, the pavement, parked cars recognisable only by their humps, one broken-down motorbike – and us.

I know John will die on this day.

Ignoring my hand under his forearm, John sits down on his favourite paisley armchair at the foot of our bed. When I lift a glass to his mouth, he purses his lips and clenches his teeth. Water dribbles down his chin. Setting the glass down, I cover his lips with mine, desperate to breathe some strength and air into him. Frantic to delay his departure from this life.

His eyelids droop and close.

The grandfather clock on the stairwell chimes eleven times. Quarter past, half past and quarter to midday.

Death comes in uninvited. We're not ready. Only a few weeks before, John took the Tube to his favourite stylist, Davey, at Harrods men's hair salon. That same evening, against his doctor's advice, he drove the car to meet me at Covent Garden to watch *Swan Lake*.

After the performance we snuggled in bed and John whistled the theme from the first scene. He read aloud the journal he kept about our trip to the Galapagos, mimicking the barks, growls and grunts of seal cows protecting their young, tapped out the frigate birds' mating dance with his fingers, and imitated the romantic rituals of blue-footed boobies.

When he read, 'Sue nearly fell into the toilet,' we both laughed a little too loudly. His hands pressing his chest, John laughed longest, and then he said, 'Don't make me laugh so much. It hurts.'

Memento mori.

After eighteen months of doctors' visits, surgery and OxyContin; after swallowing meds every few hours to deal with constipation, nausea, depression, dry mouth and profuse sweating – the side effects of the opioids and mesothelioma – John's body finally nears surrender. We're losing the battle to those asbestos threads that clasp tenaciously onto the lining of his lungs. Our hope for his remission, and the irrational belief that his cosmic journey could be delayed, sabotaged.

There are others in the room with us. Adult children whisper, get up and walk around, stroke his face, talk to him. I reach out an arm to hug, squeeze, stroke a cheek. Wipe a tear.

Chris, our palliative care doctor, whispers, 'Not long now.' He feels John's pulse, presses a stethoscope against the artery in his neck, lays a palm on his forehead. Touches my shoulder and nods.

Twelve chimes.

I sit, a sphinx, where I've been perched for hours, next to John. My right foot tingles with pins and needles. When I can no longer bear the numbness, I stretch out my legs trying not

4

to disturb him. Leaning over, I press my chapped lips on his cheek.

His warm flesh is soft and sweaty to touch, but John doesn't sigh, nod, nor blink. His jagged breathing quickens, slows and quickens again. His lungs trying to jumpstart – revving up, grinding and growling, like the sound of a car with a dying battery.

The time between each ragged breath grows longer until a protracted guttural farewell fills the air, fades and stops.

My lungs empty.

Snowflakes touch and slide down the sash window.

The room is silent. My scream, deep and throaty. I shake John's knees, hoping he'll wake, but his legs are stiff. His hands icy against my lips as heat leaves his body. No one moves. No one speaks.

'Let's lay him in bed, and you can stay with him and say your goodbyes until the undertakers get here.' Chris, eyes wet, hands shaking, has witnessed many death scenes. 'He put up a great fight…and hardly ever complained.'

A hand guides me to the bed. Everyone leaves us.

Alone.

It's the smell I remember that day before I remember the silence and the dead body.

That odour of a blocked drain that makes you retch. A smell that doesn't belong in the fickle warmth of our marital bed where John and I lie, stinking and sinking together under the load of asbestos in his shrivelled lungs.

Lying on my side, an arm over John's chest, a sharp pain shoots down my leg. Rigid, as if contaminated by John's rigor mortis, I don't stir to relieve the cramp even when a trickle of

John's warm urine touches my thigh. I suck in air – hissing, pressing my lips tightly together – and hold my breath.

My world has never been so quiet.

Air flows out of my nostrils with a whoosh. My toes curl. When I breathe in again, the smell of fish left out of the fridge for too long floats upward.

As if acknowledging my presence, John's head slips off the pillow. He rolls towards me, burping loudly. A lonely bullfrog searching for his mate. Mustard-coloured phlegm spews onto the white duvet cover. John, although officially dead, can still speak. He grunts, releasing unfamiliar fluids and gases.

Wiping the mustard crusts off my eyelashes, I turn on my side and raise myself on my elbow to look at him. He doesn't seem dead. His lips still curl up at the sides, and the familiar silver wisps of chest hair I loved to roll around my index finger poke through his pyjama jacket. The wrinkles on his forehead relax.

My hand moves to take his fingers, but they curl tight, unforgiving. The way he used to clench his fist when he was upset. My thumb and index finger wrap around his bony wrist. I lean over to touch the small scar on his chin and pull away when I scrape my palm on the white and grey bristles framing his blotchy face.

John can't have been gone long. His body still warms the bed.

I roll onto my back, staring at the 1840s moulded ceiling. Vines and leaves meander around trellises swathed with daffodils, daisies and rose blooms. Petals swirl in a large circle at the base of the glass chandelier. All I can picture are the asbestos fibres that clawed their way into spidery lungs sucking his pink flesh dry. Now as I continue to stare at the ceiling, those vines turn into vipers, striking the flowers with sharp fangs and throttling the plants with their venomous tails. Two bulbous eyes shrouded under small horns stare at me. I shiver as their scales slither around my arms and belly. I want to slip out of those damp sheets and run. Instead, I screw my eyes shut and curse.

This is a bad idea.

A gust of wind rattles the two large sash windows. The soft light from the glass chandelier hanging from the central wreath flickers. Curtains quiver.

I flop over, knocking a bottle of opiates from the bedside table. White pills scatter onto the woollen handwoven rug we bought at a market in Marrakesh. The carpet was reddish once, with Chianti stains and drops from morning cups of tea that seeped into the fabric, alerting barefoot, naked memories. But after the doctors handed John a medical death sentence, this mat turned fickle. Soaked in the smell of sour sick, sweat and urine.

In one corner of the room, John's rowing medals hang in a frame on a picture hook. Gold for a win at the Henley Regatta while a student at Imperial College; silver for a county race on the Thames, and another gold for the over thirties. Ornate brass lamps with white fringed-satin lampshades that belonged to my parents stand on our nightstand where John had stacked the spines of his bedside books: *Tinker Taylor, Soldier, Spy*; *The Man Who Mistook his Wife for a Hat*; and *The Times Crossword Puzzles*.

The books sit next to a pill tray filled with oval and round pink, blue and white pills, and orange capsules to be taken every two hours. Pink for pain, blue for constipation, white to help him sleep, brown to lift his mood, orange for multivitamins. A stack of CDs of his favourite jazz composer, John McLaughlin, spill over onto their sides. I don't ever want to listen to them again.

The stench in that bed makes me gag. The ceiling sinks lower. The vipers' jaws come closer.

I lift myself onto the pillow, taking in all the things that defined John. A favourite charcoal etching of a Gaudi portrait we bought in Barcelona; our silver-framed wedding photo on the walnut dresser; the watercolour John painted when we were in Cape Town, where thick clouds smothered Table Mountain.

Sniffling, I wipe my nose with my sleeve and pause to look at the hand-painted Armenian platter depicting the tree of life. We bought it in Jerusalem, walking on a cobbled path to the Church of the Holy Sepulchre. I study the green leaves and yellow fruit through burning eyes, hoping to find the encrypted secret: why John's chest isn't rising and falling, and why my breathing is so loud and heavy.

An impressionist-style oil painting of yellow hills, an orange-streaked sky and bronze houses with flat roofs, hangs on the wall above the headboard – a surprise wedding gift from John.

As I lie here staring at emptiness, scenes of another life butt in: crispy bacon; tan moccasins with tassels; a scarlet merino scarf; Vaughan Williams 'A Lark Ascending' – the music Johan wanted played at his memorial service.

The tartan rug on his paisley armchair, the one where he took his last breath, reminds me of a summer picnic on a field near Windsor overlooking the Thames. We sat on the soft wool enjoying roast beef sandwiches on a crunchy baguette, a bottle of chilled Chardonnay and a Thermos of tea. While cirrus clouds danced across the pale sky, John recited a few of W. H. Auden's poems about war and death. All I remember are the concrete images about an artificial wilderness, leaden skies and a man who would not live long. But the man was someone else. Not John.

Now the dead man is John.

Now the sky is leaden, the wilderness real and the air thick with an acidic, corky smell from the leftovers on the bedside table. I can taste the stale cheese sandwiches curled up at the crusts, cold cups of scummy tea with turned milk and a brown apple core.

Now there's no fresh air, nor blue skies – only an acidic, corky smell from the leftovers on the bedside table. I can almost taste the stale cheese sandwiches curled up at the crusts, cold cups of scummy tea with turned milk and a brown apple core.

Our bodies, one alive and one dead, are close but not touching. There's only one thing left for me to do. I start a one-sided conversation with John, reminding him of our plans to travel to Machu Picchu, Petra and Bhutan.

'You promised you'd never leave me. How did this happen to us?'

'I died.'

While I float in and out of reality and denial, mobile phones ring in different tones. The doorbell pierces the intermittent silence. Snow flutters, hovers and stares in at the morbid scene. The pale-grey light turns darker. A urinous yellow light from the streetlamp flutters. Wheels crunch through the snow on the street below.

I've no clue how long I've been alone with John.

Hours?

Days?

Unfamiliar feet stomp up the staircase. A loud, persistent knocking. The door handle clicks.

'The undertakers are here,' Chris says. His eyes are red, tie askew, voice hoarse.

I push my lanky hair off my forehead, stuff it into a hairband, wipe my greasy palms on my already brown-stained tracksuit trousers and grab onto John. Two strangers pry my fingers, stiff with my own rigor mortis, off his body. They lift him, place him in a black plastic bag. The zip screeches, swallowing John's blotchy face.

In those few seconds, I stare down at their cap-toed, unfashionable 'undertaker' Oxford black shoes. Shiny, polished. Whenever I see that shoe style I feel dizzy.

'Be careful, he's heavy.'

I follow them down the stairs and into the street where parked cars are covered in a white film. Only one, a black limo, stands out. Unfriendly, untouched, undisturbed. The faceless men in black wool coats stuff the floppy body bag in the trunk of the vehicle. Doors slam and wheels crunch through the snow. To the mortuary. I imagine his chest sliced open so that the pathologists and coroner can certify the cause of death.

His body has already suffered so much that the thought of further mutilation is unbearable.

I won't allow it.

I run after them, waving my arms, shouting, 'You have the wrong man.'

The hearse rounds the corner to Islington's Holloway Road.

My socks soggy, my fingers frozen, I sink onto my knees in the snow, sobbing.

It's years before I remember the other morning smell: lemon-scented soap.

But until then, I'm crushed by the illness: uncontrollable grief. Unfamiliar symptoms of mourning sickness invade my body.

CHAPTER 2

Goodbye but Not For Ever

The morning of John's cremation, I grab onto his pillow, breathe in his residue scent, crawl out on his side of the bed, and bang my knee into his bedside table. The top drawer slides open and I stare at his wallet. His initials emboss the black bifold leather, the edges frayed, the stitches unravelled. For a moment I'm uncomfortable going through his private stuff and worry that he thinks I'm being nosey. I've never gone through his wallet before. Biting my lower lip, I close my eyes for a few seconds and, hands shaking, unfold it as if I were unwrapping a fragile treasure.

In the first flap are a few ten-pound notes. In the second, his Barclays debit and Visa cards. They stare at me, daring me to get rid of them, but I defy their curse and instead of cutting the plastic up into small pieces slide them back inside. In the next flap is a navy British Airways frequent flyer card with his full name. John Donald Chadwick. Funny how his mother always called him Donald when he'd chosen to be called John at work, or Chad by his friends. I called him Chaddy.

The photo on John's driver's licence reveals a thick head of hair with a parting on the left and a fringe brushed to the side;

ears a little too small for his face; a dimpled chin; thin, straight eyebrows that turn down in a soft curve at the sides; eyes staring straight ahead into the distance. I hope he was thinking of me.

In the past year, his eyes looked troubled and sad, and his hair thinned. As the asbestos sucked him dry, his ears grew too large for his gaunt face. The almost invisible scar on his chin, from a tumble on his bike when he was a kid, protruding out of the loosening flesh.

I dig deeper into the wallet.

John's bus and Tube pass, which he used until a week before he died, sticks to the flap. I worried the physical strain of public transport would be too much for him.

'I don't want to be stuck at home like an invalid,' he said. 'I like to be with people, even if I don't know them.'

I tried not to sound schoolmarmish. 'Now, when you're in so much discomfort, why don't you take a cab?' John flinched, pulled his hands into his lap, and clenched his fist. 'You don't understand. All I want is to try to live a normal life, do normal things, and be with normal people.'

'Just do whatever you want now. Anything you want.' *Never argue with a dying husband.* I leaned over and kissed his forehead.

From the next flap, I pull out cinema ticket stubs for *Brokeback Mountain*, which we had seen a few weeks earlier. Or rather I sat there, staring at the screen and saw nothing. John seemed engrossed. We held hands all the time – a little too tight, as if knowing it would be the last movie we'd see together.

His white plastic membership card to the Royal Academy, the one he always held up and waved about as if he'd won the lottery, expires in a week. This gallery was one of John's favourite outings. He took the 91 bus, which dropped him off right outside the entrance. Recently, he viewed the Rembrandt exhibition there and came home inspired to keep painting. And he did.

'I'm going to paint until I croak,' he said.

In the attic, he sat before his easel, mixing colours, copying his favourite impressionists – Matisse and Cézanne. His colours strong and vibrant, far brighter than the originals.

His last painting was his own still life: a black vase filled with pastel-pink roses against a pale-blue background; an oily grey puddle on the white cloth under the vessel and scarlet droplets, tears rolling down the petals.

John must have sensed his end was coming. He didn't mop the dribbles or shade the petals, but moved the easel to stand right next to his rowing machine; only inches from his trainers hanging over the top of the speedometer.

Time to leave the past and get dressed for the service.

Like a naughty schoolgirl who's found out a secret, I put the wallet carefully back where I found it, trying to make it look untouched.

John chose the outfit for me to wear to his memorial ceremony – a cream blouse, brown trouser suit, and the lapis necklace he bought me for our fifth anniversary. I dress as he wished. Hiding behind a pair of Ray-Ban sunglasses, I'm unprepared for what's to come next.

In the crematorium's chilly anteroom, surrounded by family and friends, we sit on wooden benches. The coffin containing John's body, mutilated after the mandatory autopsy, flies down a chute and then turns away from us at a ninety-degree angle. Inside, he wears a white shirt with thin blue stripes, a grey wool twill suit, and a patterned navy-and-green tie that I provided the undertaker with for him.

Death has a way of driving things to consciousness, and I remember then that I forgot to give the undertaker John's underwear, socks or belt. He's not appropriately dressed. My legs tremble and won't stop, even though I press my palms on my thighs until my wrists hurt.

On cue, a small door, reminiscent of an Auschwitz oven, flies open, and John swooshes into a crimson hell. The kind of hell depicted in Michelangelo's fresco, *The Last Judgment*, at the Sistine Chapel. Flames leap up to welcome him into the 900-degree Celsius inferno. The iron door clangs shut and he's gone.

There's no going back.

In my mind's eye I see John's hair sizzling, his blood boiling, and his shrivelled lungs frying. His flesh chars, bones crumble, eyeballs shrink and curl like an egg frying in a pan. Only the asbestos fibres that sucked the life out of him survive, flying triumphantly up the crematorium chimney stack. All I have left are his ashes in a brown plastic urn.

As I carry it home on my lap, I enter the first circle of Dante's Hell, Limbo, where I remain for months. That's when I first become a stranger to myself.

I grind diligently through the symptoms of the stages of grief: depression, anger, isolation, guilt, acceptance and hope. I sob hysterically for no reason and blame myself for not keeping John alive.

All perfectly normal, I'm told. But here's the snag. There are a couple of additional stages of *mourning sickness*, that the professional shrinks – and I count myself among this group – haven't listed. I become a zombie: reckless, numb, robotic, traumatised and forgetful. Dirty laundry piles up in the bathroom. When I get to work one Monday morning, I realise that I forgot to roll on deodorant. I smell vomit.

Other, even more mysterious things happen. House keys turn up in the kitchen sink. Once I leave them in the front door overnight. I take the wrong bus or get off at the wrong Tube station. If I do head in the right direction, I can't remember what I'm supposed to be doing there.

The cashier at Sainsbury's turns to me one evening as I check out. 'What kind of dog do you have? I have a brown lab. So sweet.'

'Pardon? No, I don't have one,' I reply, rooting for my credit card.

'Oh. So, what do you do with all these cans of dog food?'

'Sorry,' I say, starting to cry. Leaving the bread, eggs, milk and dog food on the conveyor belt, I rush out. *What had I been thinking?*

Each day feels exhausting, but it's not the kind of fatigue that helps me sleep. This tiredness insists I toss and turn all night long, dozing off from time to time only to have nightmares about getting lost – either the lenses in my glasses splinter, my mobile phone's not working, or I can't find the way down the winding passage to my office. In the mornings, my eyes burn as if filled with sawdust, and my teeth feel as if covered with towelling.

I've already lost my way.

And then there's John's stuff that I stroke, smell and stare at, as if it might help bring him back: his cufflinks, shirts on hangers, paisley and striped ties on a rack, his briefcase, glasses, rowing machine, paint brushes, easel, paints, cookbooks. I hear his voice. Feel his fingers stroking my back. Smell his trainers. Use his toothbrush.

Friends talk about downsizing their homes and having less. All I want is more. They get rid of shoes and jeans, books, coffee tables and tablecloths; kitchen gadgets they don't use – juicers, panini and waffle machines; bin photo albums 'now that we have them online'; and donate CDs because 'now we can stream music from our phones'. But I want more framed photos of John; more of his music, more of his footsteps running up the stairs; more 'Hello, I'm home…' More of his sports TV shows. I want to hear the crowds shrieking at football games, cars roaring at motor rallies, and look at his sad face when his favourite team, Bolton Wanderers, loses.

If I can't have John, at least I want his possessions.

More than *want* them. I *crave* them. I develop a *hoarder disorder*.

Months after John's death, I'm still clinging to all his clutter: notebooks filled with details of our trips together, shopping lists, diaries, handwritten recipes of special dishes like roast pork and salt cod that he liked to cook, piles of bank statements, hundreds of opera CDs, theatre programmes, car and computer magazines, books of Scottish water-colourists' paintings that he copied, and old museum catalogues.

One grey day, when the never-ending drizzle pulls me into even a deeper sadness and the tears won't stop, I open his wardrobe door again, determined to start getting rid of some of John's white, pale-blue and blue-and-white-striped shirts hanging listlessly on the rail.

On one shelf, his polos and T-shirts in autumn colours,

neatly folded, look as good as new. They've a lot more life left in them. In the top drawer, his socks are rolled and stacked in four rows. I slam it shut, jamming my pinkie finger against the top.

Cursing, I jump back, angry at my clumsiness and irritated that his drawers are as always meticulous, while my bras and knickers are mushed together, and my socks more than often miss a partner. John's never do. Somehow by the time a pair of mine go into the laundry basket, the washing machine and then the dryer, one disappears. I keep the singles in the hope the real partner will turn up. Only some do.

Until he got ill John didn't feel the cold, so he only had a few sweaters. A navy merino V-neck, a few button-up cardigans in greys and blacks, and a couple of Eddie Bauer sweatshirts we bought on a recent visit to New York. Involuntarily, my face leans into the fleece, inhaling a trace of his unique scent.

I slip into the beige one at the bottom of the pile. A large man's size, it nearly reaches my knees and I roll up the sleeves to my elbow. I wear it for the rest of the day. And after I douse my wrists with his Old Spice aftershave and brush my teeth with his toothbrush, I fall asleep in it that night.

I wake up in a panic. It is well past nine. Morning light fills the bedroom, and my body feels heavy. That's mourning. Exhaustion. I am late. Very late for work.

Another pathological symptom that emerges is 'avoidance coping'.

Simple tasks like shopping drain me. One Sunday, when I force myself to at least try to buy some fruit and vegetables at Islington's street market, I forget what I'm supposed to be doing there. Picking up a tangerine, I close my eyes and rub my thumbs over the crepe-textured skin cocooned in the palms of my hands. My fingers slide over the peel, caressing each ridge and wrinkle. I lift the fruit to my nose and breathe in, long and deep, hoping the sharp citrus scent might bring John back to me.

'Such a lovely man, we do miss him,' calls Bob, the vendor from our favourite stall. 'I loved our chats.' He stands under a canvas awning behind his table, filling baskets with apples, pears and oranges. He wipes his hands on a blue-and-white checked apron and looks at me. 'Gonna rain any minute…fed up with this grey…got a brolly with you? You doing okay, luv?'

I start to tell Bob that I'm settling down all right, but I can't find the words to pretend. My fists clench the tangerine, suddenly aware of the juice trickling down my forearms and inside my shirtsleeves.

Bob leans over the table and touches my wrists. 'It gets better, luv,' he says, trying to look into my tear-filled eyes, but I can't meet his gaze. He continues to pile apples, oranges, potatoes and broccoli in baskets, tempting me to fill my own shopping bag, but then I remember. There's only one of us now.

On Saturday mornings, John and I enjoyed shopping for our fruit and vegetables at this market together. We picked shiny Granny Smith apples, breathed in the aroma of fresh parsley and celery, and scooped handfuls of beans and Brussel sprouts into brown paper bags for Bob to weigh. But it was my John who always chose the citrus, rubbing the tips of his fingers over the dimpled skin. Each week he'd describe the colour as if it were sacred. To him, it was almost holy.

'The colour this week is deeper,' or 'it's almost reddish,' or 'almost lemony,' he'd say.

As a child, it was an orange that brought colour into his life for the very first time. John grew up in the forties in Bolton, a cotton-milling town near Manchester. He described never-ending grey skies with smoke billowing from chimney stacks and soot smothering oak trees and privet hedges. Stray cotton threads – a soporific haze, dank and dim – infiltrated people's lungs, fuelling hacking coughs.

'Food rationing continued after the Second World War and everything we ate was pale,' John said when we first met. 'We ate white bread with margarine the colour of glue; beige Spam and sallow powdered scrambled eggs along with boiled potatoes, cabbage and turnips. When I was seven, I saw my first orange,' John said. 'And it was if I saw colour for the first time.'

My childhood was nothing like his. In South Africa, I grew up with plenty of sunlight, purple jacaranda trees and crimson and magenta bougainvillea. All kinds of produce filled the fruit and vegetable stores: papayas, bananas, apricots, mangoes and mulberries; tomatoes, pumpkins, broccoli and courgette. It was difficult to think of life with ashen skies and bland food. My heart filled with compassion for the boy John, deprived of such simple delights.

'One of our neighbours bought one orange,' John said. 'It was a spectacle – we'd heard about it, but never seen or eaten one. They put the fruit on their kitchen table, and every day all us neighbours crowded in to marvel at it. We could only stare at it. No one was allowed to touch it. After a week, the skin turned grey and mouldy. No one suggested peeling it to look inside, and worse, no one even tasted it.'

Decades later, every time we came home from our Saturday market shopping, the first thing John did was slice into an orange.

Eating citrus was a divine experience, tangible proof that he was no longer that boy stuck in a polluted, war-exhausted town.

Now, months after John's death, I stand on the bustling market street holding that tangerine, as if John is here with me, cradled against my lips. I almost hear him and Bob discussing the Brexit shenanigans as he pays for our purchases.

I grab onto a support at Bob's market stall to steady myself, place the squishy tangerine back onto the table, turn away and back onto the street. Smells of pungent mushrooms, leeks, onions and garlic from a nearby stall follow me. Back on the main road, a drizzle drips down the back of my neck. I walk home with an empty shopping basket.

More *mourning* sickness.

For months I suffer from *phantasmagoria*...illusions.

John stands with his back to me, hanging onto a pole on the Tube. When I call his name, a man with a goatee and bushy eyebrows turns around and stares. I run after John when I see him walking across Hyde Park or Trafalgar Square. When I reach him, his lips are too flabby or too mean, his eyes are the wrong colour, his chin too pointy. My world is filled with all the wrong faces that look nothing like him.

And I suffer from *incarcerophobia*, even though the prison is of my own making.

When I come home from work in the evenings, I open and then shut the small black wrought-iron gate leading up the concrete stairs to the entrance of our London home. It clangs shut behind me and I voluntarily walk up the three stairs, open the front door, and step into my prison cell.

I'm scared of being here in solitary.

One drizzly evening, the key in my cold fist refuses to slide into the front door lock, as if it knows that only pain awaits on the other side. My fingers lose any sense of feeling. My hand shakes. It takes me a while to realise that I have to turn it the right way up to face the deadbolt lock.

Inside the dark entrance hall, I trip over a pile of envelopes. Garish junk mail from local restaurants advertising curry and pizza; and a stack of *Guardian* newspapers that's been lying there for weeks. I regain my balance, but the contents of my tote spew out onto the floor – a rattail comb with a few lost teeth, my leather purse, my cheque book with a torn plastic cover, a tube of plum-coloured lipstick and a crumpled pack of soggy Kleenex.

The grandfather clock chimes eight and an unwelcome silence greets me. No footsteps come down the stairs; no cork pops out of a bottle of Chardonnay, and no jazzy strains of John Coltrane or Stan Getz filter in from the living room. I sniff, hoping to breathe in aromas of rosemary-roasted chicken, garlic bread or grilled asparagus, but the air smells musty.

No lips kiss mine and there's no snugly chest to hug. My forefinger traces my cracked lips in an effort to keep John's kisses with me. Rivulets from my damp hair trickle under my collar and down my spine; I shake my head as if I were a wet dog after a drenching.

When I flip on the light switch, only shadows fill the hall. My steaming breath is the only warmth. The frigid gloom reminds me of the letter in the crimson-striped envelope that I ripped open a few weeks ago, informing me that I'd defaulted on the electricity payments.

A shrouded streetlight spills pools of sickly amber on the mahogany dining table. I make out a mound of scrunched-up

Kit-Kat wrappers; a bottle of Tylenol; a mountain of papers that are probably important because of the logos in in the corners – Barclays Bank, Thames Water, Visa; and a bundle of cards with roses and birds covered with kind messages of commiseration – comforting tear-stained notes that I'd read again and again, breaking and mending my heart all at the same time. Each one needs to be answered with a personal response. I can't look at them anymore. But neither can I bin nor box them. Friends, neighbours, family members and work colleagues have expressed how sorry they are for my loss.

But John isn't lost – I am.

I'm crippled by *mazeophobia,* a fear of getting lost.

I lose everything: my patience, my sense of humour and the memories of all the wonderful times John and I had together. Losing focus, I can no longer write client proposals or listen to board presentations. Paging through the A–Z, I wander aimlessly, searching for client offices I've visited several times before. Even finding the supermarket checkout counter is more difficult than navigating the Hampton Court Maze.

Standing in the dark kitchen, I kick off my sodden leather boots. There's just enough light coming in from the street to glare at my other companions: A carton of curdled milk in the sink, a bruised Granny Smith apple on top of the gas hob and a slice of fossilised toast still in the toaster.

Shivering, I rummage through kitchen drawers and find a box of matches and a short candle, once used for romantic dinners. I melt the bottom of the candle and glue it to the bottom of a cereal bowl. Dinner would be baked beans again, straight out of the tin, but tonight they would be cold without the crunchy wholemeal toast and a cup of tea. Collapsing on a three-legged barstool, I force myself to eat the salty-sugary nuggets smothered in gooey tomato sauce.

Leaving the spoon sticking out of the tin of partially eaten mush, I take off my trench coat and drape it over the stool to dry. In Dickensian manner, I pick up the bowl and, balancing the candle, follow the flame one agonising step after another up the stairs to the bathroom on the second floor. The cold from the icy floor tiles stings my soles through damp tights. I skip brushing my teeth and removing makeup, blow out the candle, run into our bedroom, and slip out of my skirt. I slide off my bra from beneath my polar neck sweater, throw my jacket over the duvet for added warmth, and dive under the covers. The sheets feel like frozen cardboard.

Maybe it's exhaustion, denial or my paper-thin bedclothes, but for a few moments I forget that John died two months ago. I wriggle closer to his side of the bed, stretch out my arm to wrap around his chest. Instead, my palm grazes the valve of an empty oxygen tank.

John's physical presence is everywhere. His Gordon Ramsey cookbook, his merino scarf on the dining room chair, his mobile phone next to the landline. The daffodil bulbs John planted in the window box outside the kitchen sprout small yellow buds on green stalks. They crane their necks into the window looking for him, but the shrivelled African violets on the indoor bookshelf give up the search and lose their blooms. Dandelions shoot up in the cracks between paving stones in the back garden. The rose bushes sprout gangly shoots.

Monophobia. Ignored and unloved.

All around me people go out for coffee, drinks and dinner, laughing and chatting as if nothing has changed. Locked in this bleak vestibule of my own making, I keep myself isolated and insulated, hoping that one day I'll meet up with John again. I grab onto the shopping trolley in the supermarket to hold myself steady when I hear his favourite song – Coltrane's 'My One and Only Love' – and often eat bacon which I don't particularly like, just to hear his sighs of delight.

My hope is the wrong kind of hope. It's irrational but I don't fight it anymore.

Finally, I accept that crazy is okay as long as no one else knows. When I visit my doctor for my annual check-up, she wants to prescribe Prozac. Overwhelmed by *pharmacophobia,* and all the pills John had to swallow, I never want to swallow a pill again. Everyone I know seems to be taking something: sleeping pills, anti-depressants, headache pills, multi-vitamins, or something for indigestion, cholesterol or high blood pressure. I'd probably have been better off if I'd been taking them too.

Work and yoga get me out of bed in the mornings. I view them as non-intrusive medication, proud that I'm not swallowing any meds. That's when I realise I need a change. Or maybe I need *to* change.

The only problem is, I don't know how.

My only question is, can I learn?

LOST

CHAPTER 3

He's Always There

His shoes come into focus first. Tan loafers with tassels. I'd been with him in Harrods when he'd bought them. His right leg crosses over the left – swinging rhythmically. The way they do when he's happy. He drapes his arm across the backrest of the park bench and caresses another woman's cheek.

Betrayal.

The man who is John puts his arm around the woman's shoulders and pulls her towards him.

The fragrant pines and spring blooms bring back sensuous memories. Walks in gardens and forests, and generous kisses enveloped in a bouquet of pungent wild mushrooms and violet bluebells. John's fingers fondling the back of my neck.

She, whoever she is, snuggles into the man. Her blonde curls flow down his chest. He pushes his tweed cap – the one I gave him as an impulse gift a few months ago – back off his forehead. His hands are in full view. I can almost feel his long fingers sneaking up under my sweater and stroking my breasts. I try to breathe, but my throat is blocked.

In Regent's Park, I no longer see the purple rhododendrons, glistening in the spring sunshine. Orange azaleas fade into a grey background. Fragrance from the pine trees wafts away. Raucous crows go quiet. Geese fly across the pale-blue sky in perfect formation. They glide down one at a time onto the grass and feed in a nearby pond where water gushes out of the mouths of babes on a bronze fountain. Airplanes send white smoke streaks across the clear blue sky, buses and cabs grumble in the distance, and the earth quivers beneath my feet as underground trains rattle through tunnels.

Why are John and that *woman* laughing? The laugh isn't his laugh. When did he start to laugh like that? John doesn't chortle – his contagious laugh rumbles up from his belly.

A breeze blows into my face. Stray locks of hair fall out of my topknot and over my eyes. I tuck the greasy strands behind my ears and wipe the oily residue onto the back of my jeans. John loves the scent of my jasmine shampoo; I wish I had washed and styled my hair before coming out. Nudging my glasses up the bridge of my nose, I pick up my pace.

My foot slips on a step. I try to regain my balance and fall. *Hard.* My knees hit the ground. Then my chest. My glasses crunch as I fall flat on my face. The jagged concrete grazes my knees, and warm blood trickles out of my nose. I wonder how many bones I've broken.

'Are you okay?' a deep male voice asks. 'That was some fall.'

The husky voice is so familiar, but why is he speaking with an American accent? I try to answer, but can't force the words out. Straining my neck, I look up. The world is a blur, but I see the cuff of his corduroys. The ones I ironed. Enough to know it's really him.

'Can we help you up?' The stranger interrupts my reverie.

'Just give me a few minutes,' I say, lifting my head. 'I'm

winded, that's all. I'll be all right.'

Someone touches my shoulder. It must be John.

He's back…he's back…he's back, my internal voice repeats.

But the hand feels too light. The voice drawls too much. My stomach churns. Bile oozes into my mouth.

'Your glasses are scratched, and the frame is bent. Can you see at all?' He rests his palm on my shoulder.

My thinking is irrational. Such is the effect of my illusion. Eyes wide open. A somnambulist, I see a slab of concrete, smell stale cigarette smoke, hear him breathing.

With the stranger's arm under my right hand, I ease myself upright and stagger to my feet. How gently he touches my wrist, pulsing with pain. My heart thumps loudly enough for him to hear. Logic and fantasy fold together.

I scrunch up my nose and squint at the stranger. His hair is fine, almost sparse, with no streaks of grey like John's. The man's thin lips replace John's sensual smiling mouth. What am I thinking? Yet I let myself dream on to see where it will take me. My imagination carries me into a wild hypothesis.

Don't be ridiculous, I chastise myself, *John died!*

My knees and head throb, my palms sting where the skin scraped off. My lungs burn.

'I can't believe I'm so clumsy,' I say, holding a tissue under my nose to soak up the blood. 'I guess I just missed that step.'

Insincere. What I really want to say is that I think the stranger is my dead husband. I paste on a false smile.

'I'm glad you're okay,' the man says, letting go of my arm. I stare down again at his shoes. Yes, the very same tan moccasins with tassels that John wore.

'Thank you for helping. I'm so sorry to have disturbed

you.' I wish he could stay a bit longer.

He nods. 'You okay? You look all shook up. Like you've just seen a ghost.'

If only I could tell him.

I smile and nod, and the stranger walks back to the bench. He whispers to his companion. She turns to look at me as if I'm someone she knows. *The man's former wife?*

Three months after the first anniversary of John's death, this loving couple tugs me into an emotional twister. *How much longer will I keep getting so upset?* Normally a rational, logical person, I'm scared I might be losing it. How will I ever convince myself that John will never be back?

Folly.

The joyous fragrance of spring evaporates. Purple and pink blooms fade. Regent's Park is stark and bare. I still struggle to believe he's gone for good.

When I reach home, I sink into the sofa and close my eyes.

I think back to one week ago on Rivington Pike, a hilltop near Bolton, where John grew up. It's on this hill that John requested I scatter his ashes. I opened the urn just as it began to drizzle and slipped my hand inside. Grabbing a handful of sticky remains, I threw John up into the air. On that blustery spring afternoon charred flakes flew back into my face and onto my lips. Salty, clinging, persistent. The sticky particles remained glued to the palm of my hand.

Isn't it time to get to grips with reality and be done with the denial?

I sink into the billowy cushions and kick off my trainers without opening the laces. Blood stains the knees of my pale-blue jeans. My lenses are scratched, frames distorted; my palms burn and my head pounds. Loamy, evocative spring smells return. *Leave me alone.* But the memories refuse. I doze off to a world where young bluebell stems crunch beneath my back and John's lips explore my belly button.

Coming to terms with the death of my beloved husband is complicated by a steadfast belief that John will return. I haven't stopped looking for auspicious signs that might lead me to him. I find myself sharing things with him that I know he'd relish. On a Paris vacation two years after his passing, I invite his phantasm to a tea parlour near the Bois de Boulogne and order his favourite patisserie – a Napoleon cake consisting of layers of puff pastry interlaced with a rich custard filling. With each bite I take, I feel him licking his lips with joy.

John is always with me.

Even when he's not.

CHAPTER 4

Midnight in Mumbai

Monsoon smells. Mould, mosquito fogging, overflowing sewers and exhaust fumes overwhelm the scent of my own naivety, despair and confusion.

Monsoon sounds. Honking buses, car doors slamming, rain pounding against tin roofs. Thunder mumbling, grumbling and exploding as if cannonballs are flying across the heavens.

Monsoon sights. At the exit of Mumbai's international airport, drivers huddle under a plastic corrugated roof, brandishing white placards with the names of their passengers. In the small pick-up area, people hug and kiss, slap backs and stuff bulging suitcases into car boots. Rickshaws slice through the traffic. One man in a long beige Nehru jacket bends down to kiss the feet of a much older man with a long white beard. Lightning splays across the sky, forking in every direction. The world blurs through steamy glasses. I run my sleeve across them until I can see the crowds, six or seven deep, pressing against the railings.

I, a pillar of salt, can't move. People push past me, muttering that I'm blocking the exit. I stand, paralysed.

Move!

I straighten up and force myself to shove on when the front wheel of my baggage trolley wedges in a crack in the pavement. Leaning against the handle, I throw my weight against it until the trolley finally judders forward. The top suitcase falls victim to a murky puddle at my feet. Bending over to heave up the bag, I feel my tote slip off my shoulder and try to grab it. Too late. A tube of crimson lipstick, a hairbrush, a few crumpled tissues and a leather purse stuffed with sterling bank notes and a few credit cards spill out onto the ground.

I bend over, scoop everything back into the bag and root around for my passport. Not there.

'Please…please,' I mumble, praying to no one. My fingers wrap around a familiar oblong shape. *Yes, yes. Thank you!* I lift my delinquent suitcase back on top of the other.

A man yells, 'Taxi, taxi,' only a few inches from my face.

I cringe, step back and stumble over my own feet. My soaked jacket squishes with each step. One black stiletto heel sinks into a crack between two concrete slabs. I pull on my foot, but nothing moves. When I bend down and tug, the shoe doesn't budge. Holding onto the heel with one hand, I yank it. The leather scrapes off. Serves me right for wearing such silly Jimmy Choos.

On vacation to Kerala with John six years earlier, we laughed at the blaring horns, squealing tyres and spirited slaps on the back as we inhaled the heady scent of Brylcreem mixed with sandalwood. I hadn't choked on or even noticed the clouds of black exhaust fumes then, and John hadn't struggled to breathe.

This time I'm here on my own. Cowering. Intimidated by the cacophony. Time to turn round and go straight back home. Now.

A trolley slams into my ankle. A sharp pain shoots up the back of my leg.

I let out a yelp.

A woman in a blue-and-scarlet sari stares through me as if I don't exist before weaving past me. I stop and close my eyes, button up my jacket and try to calm myself. Deep breath in, slow exhale.

Another bolt of lightning dissects the sky.

I've read novels about monsoons, watched movies like *Monsoon Wedding* with its violent storms, but I've never imagined what it would be like to stand in a black trouser suit in the midst of the downpour – my flat-ironed bob frizzing, my shoes ruined and woollen jacket sodden. I shake my head as if I've just stepped out from a waterfall.

If I'm going to make it here, I have to stop being so naïve.

I don't remember sleeping much that first year after John died, but I do remember the dreams. John calling my name, John reaching out a hand, John snoring gently next to me. Most mornings my head hung over the foot of the bed and my feet pressed against the headboard. Cappuccino at the Ritz, where I often met with clients over breakfast, tasted soapy. At weekends I watched our favourite programmes *Inspector Morse* and *Sex in the City*, drinking a little too much Chianti, and forgetting the plot. I tried walking, reading, visiting friends and family, and imagining John's hand on my knee as I watched *Swan Lake*, my favourite ballet, at Sadler's Wells. I left at the interval.

When colleagues insisted that we get together for drinks after work, I tried to laugh and join the banter. I did try. I pasted a false smile on my face. Even so, when a client based in

Mumbai offered to hire me to build a strong leadership team for their retail business, I declined.

'You've got nothing to keep in you London now,' the CEO insisted. 'We'd like you to come and coach the team for a year, or maybe two.'

I declined again.

Just as I was leaving the office one Friday evening, a large FedEx envelope arrived from India. I read and re-read the job offer four or maybe five times over the weekend. Finally, after a long chat with my children, I initialled the bottom of each page, and signed on the dotted line at the end.

The following Monday, I met with the CEO of our coaching firm and told him I was leaving.

'You're giving up your partner status?' my boss asked, tugging at one ear. 'You're leaving the firm when the coaching practice you worked so hard to build is now a thriving business?'

'Yes, I know,' I whispered, wiping my eyes with the back of my hand. 'But I think a change of scenery will do me good.'

'You're leaving everything.' He rubbed his palms together and stared at his laptop. 'Have you thought of taking a couple of weeks, or maybe months off?'

I twisted a paper clip in my lap and tried to speak. But all I could do was dab my eyes with a tissue and smear mascara across the back of my hand. He was not sympathetic. He said my clients might leave the practice. I nodded.

'You need a coach yourself,' he said rocking on his office chair. 'We need at least a month's notice.' He stood up, opened the door and motioned me to leave.

I opened my mouth to tell him I'd stay, but instead I walked into an icy-white passage. I fretted that I was making a mistake. I changed my mind. Again. Then, with a momentum of its own, the move happened quickly. Within a few weeks, I rented out our – now *my* – home, packed up and stored our linen, crockery and cutlery, sorted out bank accounts and mail-forwarding services, organised a work permit and had rabies, typhoid and cholera vaccinations.

I couldn't get over the shock of what I'd done. But this was a good omen.

Preparing for the move helped me put an end to stroking John's clothes and wearing his jackets and ties, sweaters and socks. I folded them in bin bags and took them to the local charity store. But his toothbrush and razor came with me to India.

At Mumbai's airport exit, I look out across a sea of women dressed in yellow, purple, jade and orange saris, and shalwar kameeze – long tunics over baggy trousers. My suitcase is full of all the wrong clothes – black, beige and navy jackets, trousers and tight skirts, nylon stockings, a thick faux fur coat and sheepskin boots. A plastic bag in the second case is filled with bottles of anti-malaria tablets, four boxes of tampons, several tubes of toothpaste and enough shampoo and conditioner, deodorant and moisturiser to last a family of five for six months. So many people warned me how hard it is to get these products in Mumbai, but I should've done more research: later I learn you can buy them all here.

Just beyond the barrier at the exit, people crane their necks to check for a familiar face, raising white placards with black lettering. I search for mine amongst dozens of others as I walk past unfamiliar names: Mr Gupta, J. Winston, Mrs Mohan, Canara Bank and Ashish Bhattacharya – but I can't find mine.

My glasses steam up and I keep wiping them with the bottom of my blouse. A man bumps into my elbow.

'You needing taxi?'

'No, thank you,' I say, trying to convince myself that's true. 'My driver is here, somewhere.'

I back away from the barrier and straighten up. No one is here for me. I release the handle of my baggage trolley and lean forward, relying on my elbows to prop me up, and ignoring the people shouting at me to get out of the way. Slumped over the top of my suitcase I remember the words of Rama, my new boss, and straighten up.

'Don't worry,' he'd said. 'There will be a driver at the airport for you and he'll take you to your hotel.'

I decide to make one more round before going back inside the terminal to try to find someone with a phone to call Rama. No doubt he won't be happy to be woken up past midnight, but what if I have no choice?

Now I'm convinced I've done the wrong thing. Running away from London to India won't help me get over my loss. Wherever I try to hide, I'll feel the same.

No John. No joy.

I made many promises to John over the years. Promises to love, cherish and adore in sickness and in health. Promises to stay with him through that asbestos journey in the valley of death. Promises to keep him at home and not ship him off to a hospice. That his last dinner would be his favourite foods – sole meunière grilled in parsley butter, boiled new potatoes, green string beans and garlic bread, accompanied by a bottle of Pinot Grigio. For dessert, chocolate profiteroles served with apple brandy.

I promised him a humanist memorial ceremony, and that his ashes would be scattered on Rivington Pike, that hill near Bolton where he rode his bike as a kid. I promised that the memorial ceremony would be invitees only made up from a list he'd prepared personally. I also promised him I wouldn't give up on myself when he was gone.

'You'll have to live on for the both of us,' John said, 'promise me.'

But I'm beginning to think that last promise is one I won't be able to keep. I have an urge to turn around and bolt straight back home.

My Indian welcome committee consists of bumping into strangers' bodies, breathing in smoky pollution and the wet, acrid odour of my own wretchedness. This is not a good start. But I owe it to John to try again. After all, given that I'd no clue how to be a caregiver or to deal with the unknown demands of mesothelioma, I'd come this far on my own.

Advice from ambulance-chasing friends, colleagues and family – all well-meaning – I dismissed as unhelpful. They didn't seem to understand what John and I were really going through. Looking back now, I think I was just angry at anyone who didn't have a terminally ill family member at home. My cheeks burn at my arrogance. All I could think about back then was us. All I think about now is me. Me and my loss.

I wrap my palms firmly around the handle of the baggage trolley and swivel it around. One last effort to retrace my footsteps through a sprawling semicircle around the white placards waving like flags of surrender to the pummelling rain. I squint at the names again. Gupta; Tata; Collins; Barclays; Madan; Wipro…but mine still isn't there.

I push my drenched hair up off my face and away from my eyes. My glasses are streaked. My patience is gone. Then I see the sign: MAD S. BLOTCH. *Well, what do you know*, I think. A new name and new identity to help me keep that promise to John.

Raising one hand to let my driver know I'm here, I fight off the urge to laugh as I often do when I'm nervous or excited. Or relieved. 'Mad S. Blotch,' I say to no one in particular. Yes, I probably am.

A slim, short man wearing a white shirt with navy epaulets, holding my name high, shrugs his shoulders, frowns, and looks away as he lowers the card. This man who is to be my driver appears oblivious to my presence. I shout out and poke at my chest with my finger. 'Hello!' I call again, louder this time, as I wave frantically.

Suddenly, his eyes widen and he shoves his way through the crowd. 'A veeery big velcome to India, *merrim*,' he says. He wears a name tag on his chest. I squint at it.

'Namaste, Khamat, thank you for coming to get me.' Namaste is the one word I learned at yoga and one of the few Hindi words I know.

'I am getting so verrry worried not seeing you,' Khamat shouts above another thunder ball. 'I'm thinking you must be a man, so I'm not looking for a lady.'

I smile. 'I'm pleased to meet you.'

Holding an umbrella over my head, he shrugs and glances up at the skies. 'It ees a big monsoon today,' he says, and wheels the baggage trolley through the downpour to the parking lot.

I follow him through the maze of people and taxis until he stops at a car, opens the back door and motions me in. My thighs squish against the plastic-covered seat. I stick my fingers into the cracks and fumble for the seat belt.

'No, *merrim,* no seat belts, very sorry, but me, I'm a very good driver.' He shuts my door and ducks into the driver's seat. 'Now I'm taking you to Taj Hotel in Colaba.'

Relieved not to be on my own, I thank him. No need to make a fuss about safety now. I pull my Fodor's Essential India guidebook from my tote, open the folded corner with a map of Mumbai, and try to find the route we'll take to the city's southern tip. There's only one main artery, The Western Express.

Khamat accelerates out of the parking area into the heavy traffic and brakes suddenly to avoid a mother with a baby in one arm and a child's hand on the other. A few minutes later, a cart some eight metres long, laden with piles of wooden logs, veers straight toward us from the opposite direction. The car skids sideways as Khamat brakes again. I fly forward against the front seat. Khamat seems unperturbed. My neck cricks and I curse softly, rolling my head from side to side until I'm sure I'm okay. A skinny man strains to get the wheels of his barrow out of a pothole in the road. The cart sways from side to side. I hold my breath, prepared for the worst, until I realise that Khamat hoots at everyone, more often to warn people that his car is there than to goad them into moving. The man lifts the corner of his loincloth, tucks it in around his waist, and leans into the barrow. Finally, the cart lurches to the left and then the right before lunging forward, logs intact.

I glance at my watch. Three a.m. Mumbai is still a humming hive of activity. The Western Express is bogged down with trucks and buses like the M25 during rush hour.

'Now is the time when the call centres are changing shifts. Too many buses,' Khamat says, turning around to see if I understand.

'Is there a time when the city isn't so busy?'

'Always busy. You see, *merrim*, the big trucks bringing fruits and vegetables, and gas balloons, water and petrol…they can only come into the city between midnight and seven o'clock in the morning, so at night it's very much busy also.'

The car crawls along, dodging potholes, motorbikes and pedestrians weaving from one side of the road to the other. Music blares from radios trying to drown out the barrage of incessant honking and raucous rain. Children, adults and babies sleep on the pavement under sheets of plastic. Some lie on tables, others on wooden planks on top of a few stones or bricks to lift them off the ground. One man lies with a baby sleeping on his chest and an older child curled under his arms. Trucks, vans and the wheels of our car splash water over them. The city's drains choke under the deluge. I gag at the smell of urine.

This is Mumbai. I realise suddenly that I'm far, far from my comfort zone. A few hours later Khamat turns into the driveway of a hotel entrance framed by neo-classical, Corinthian columns. Eastern rhythms blare out across the marble lobby. Chattering women in silk saris of mauve, plum, indigo and crimson appear with rows of gold bangles and large emerald-and-sapphire necklaces. Men in charcoal Nehru jackets, beige churidars and pink scarves mingle in small groups. Khamat helps me out of the car, and I walk up to the black marble desk to check in. A few minutes later, I take a deep breath as I slide the plastic key into the lock of my tenth-floor home away from home.

The same haunting silence that filled our bedroom when John took his last breath greets me. There is no distinction. My loss has stalked me all the way to India. Without brushing my teeth, I flop onto the crisp white bedding aching to hear John react with some smart quip. Like the time after his surgery when he'd smeared his toast thick with butter and we'd childishly lost the seriousness of the moment.

'At least I don't have to worry about cholesterol now,' John said. 'I can eat all the bacon, butter and chocolate I want.'

Lying on my back on the king-sized bed, I stare at the contemporary flat ceiling. It is so very different from the 1840s coved ceiling in our London home, which I remember staring at as I lay in bed with my dead John waiting for the undertaker. The intricate mural – the vines and leaves meandering around trellises swathed with daffodils, daisies and rose blooms, the petals swirling in a large circle at the base of the glass chandelier. The vines that turned into vipers daring me to die right along with him.

I shiver, as if the reptile of death is slithering around my arms and belly. And at some point during the night, exhausted from fear and my travels to a new world, I fall into a deep torpor. And dream. Bad dreams.

I wake to early morning light streaming through the slit between the curtains. My eyelids feel heavy under the image of the asbestos fibres that clung to John's spidery lungs as they sucked on his pink flesh.

After showering and breakfasting on papaya and curd, chai, a masala omelette filled with onions, tomatoes and chilli, I find Khamat standing smiling at the hotel entrance, waiting to drive to the office.

'You had your breakfast?' he enquires as he escorts me to the car.

'Yes. Thank you for asking, Khamat. And you?'

He ignores my question. I learn only weeks later that, like so many other Indians, he eats only one meal a day – lunch, supplemented by a banana or snack.

'We only have thirty ks to go,' he says, 'so we will be there in some time.' I can't help but think he sounds more than a little like a tour guide.

'This is the St Pancras,' Khamat says, pointing at a once-grand, now grimy building adorned by quirky ornaments. The gargoyles with grotesque faces, stained-glass windows, spires, turrets, domes and gables built in a Gothic architectural style are similar to, but more ornate than London's St Pancras, where John and I parted many a morning on our separate commutes to work. Grief drives memories to the surface.

My throat feels as if it has a rag stuffed down it. The red paisley silk kerchief – the one he tucked into the top pocket of his jacket on our wedding day – is tied in a knot onto the handle of my tote. As Khamat takes a corner, I dab at my eyes, only to see the station's ornate façade vanish replaced by the brick walls of London's Golders Green crematorium and John's memorial service. For a few minutes I no longer hear the rain pounding down against the car roof. I jump when Khamat hammers the horn with his fist. An elderly hunchback man shuffles faster. I press John's kerchief against my cheek and wipe my eyes again as I try to focus on what Khamat is saying.

'You know, *merrim*, the Britishers, they built this station for Queen Victoria in 1887.' He has to shout over the din. 'You see, India was part of the British Empire. They build good stations and railroads. For a long time now, we have our own country,' he adds with disguised pride. 'That is very good, but no one is looking after the buildings. Too much black mould from too much pollution.'

I nod but don't speak. Coming from London, I'm aware there must be plenty of anti-British sentiments in the country. The colonial masters pillaged gold, coal, emeralds, marble and spices during their reign, and levied heavy taxes.

I look at the front windshield and the wipers swishing back and forth. Gridlock. Everyone is at a standstill for as far as I can see.

Khamat switches off the car engine. I study the idiosyncratic building that shows all the complexities of an Indian palace, with its Italian design and the conqueror's vision. On top of a column to one side of the main entrance squats the statue of a lion. On the other side, a tiger. The structure looks if the British architect was determined to control the sunlight and design while working with local craftsmen and materials to nurture their buildings' unique motifs and symbols.

'Now we need to move,' Khamat says, starting the car and shifting the gears.

He veers onto the pavement to overtake the cars in front, scraping and knocking over a metal table loaded with branches of bananas. He doesn't stop to check on the damage or to help the vendor who raises his arms, yells, lifts the table, and begins restacking his wares.

Khamat shows no concern, and although I want to tell him to stop and help the vendor, I don't. I feel bad. At least I could have offered some money to compensate him for his loss.

Three hours later, we turn off the rutted and tarred street

onto a wide gravel road. Stones thump incessantly against the side of the car. By now, the shock absorbers, just like my spine, have blown apart. With each jolt, my head bumps against the car roof. I find myself picking at the skin around the cuticle of my right thumb. And then gnawing at it. My meeting with the company's CEO was scheduled to start an hour ago. Once, I might have been in my element as a traveller in an awkward situation and laughed it off. Now I feel incompetent, unsteady, not at all sure what I'm doing here. Not even able to get to work on time…on my very first day.

Rickshaws bounce all around us, moving nearly as fast as we…as the car creeps along. Finally, we pull to a stop aside a modern, portentous arched gateway. 'This is your office,' Khamat announces, mopping his forehead with a handkerchief.

Besieged by people, buses, bikes, rickshaws and motor scooters, the white arch jolts me into yet another world. From a shack a few yards away, an aroma of sugary bananas and samosas wafts by. I'm hungry again.

There's no choice but to slosh though muddy puddles and shove my way through the unfamiliar chaos to get inside the building and onto the slick marble floors. It's unexpectedly quiet, but not silent.

'Good morning, madam,' a man at the entrance presses his palms together at his chest and bows his head, 'Shree Rama is waiting for you. I am Girish, his assistant.'

'Namaste, Girish,' I say, running my fingers through my hair, hoping my mascara isn't smudged. 'It's a pleasure to meet you.'

As I take in the broad-brush modern art on the walls, a chaiwallah rushes to push a cup of tea into my hand. The hot, sweet drink helps me regain some emotional balance and my hand stops shaking. The spacious entrance is filled with four Ficus plants, or rather shrubs, in large clay pots that reach up to my waist. A row of purple and white orchids standing on a broad teak windowsill fill the area with gentle fragrance that reminds me of the hot house at Kew Gardens.

Conscious of the perspiration settling in my waistband, I follow Girish to the meeting room where my future colleagues have been waiting for over an hour. I'm convinced they'll fire me on day one and send me back to London. If I fail here there'll be nowhere else to run and nowhere else to hide.

'Rama will be here in a few minutes,' Girish says, rubbing the back of his neck with the palm of his right hand. 'He is on a call, but knows you're here. Bad traffic, eh?'

Flushed and scarcely able to breathe, I nod and smile. 'I had no idea it would take so long to get here. Many apologies.'

'You'll soon get used to Bombay traffic.' My first lesson in cultural integration…locals still use the city's old name.

While we wait for Rama, I walk around the room, shaking hands, and making an attempt to remember names and job titles. The team of ten men are in their thirties, or maybe forties, with MBAs, leaving me feeling unqualified for the post.

The room goes quiet as Rama walks in booming, 'Susan, welcome to Bombay traffic, we are happy to see you.' He towers over me and pumps my hand. 'Team, please welcome our new team member from London. As you know, she's joining us as our in-house guru coach.'

Rama pulls out the empty chair next to his at the head of the table. 'Please,' he says and nods to the team. Plush office chairs scrape against the stone floor, but no one speaks.

My hands won't stop shaking even though I tuck then under my thighs. I hope he won't notice.

'You have all read Susan's bio.' He turns to face me and places a hand on my shoulder.

'Susan, welcome. We are very glad that you've joined our team…'

I don't feel like an expert. Has he oversold me, the only senior female expat to the team?

Engrossed in my own self-ruin, I don't hear the rest of Rama's introduction or the team clapping. I don't see him smile, nor notice the silence in the room as my colleagues wait for me to speak. Pressure builds up behind my eyes and I close them for a few seconds before I make the introductory speech I prepared.

John whispers in my ear, 'They're waiting, go for it.'

This is it, I think. *This is my new home. My new team.*

But I'm still in a faraway country.

CHAPTER 5

An Intruder Meets His Match

Night Two in Mumbai

Crash!

I bolt upright, clasping my pillow to my chest.

What...what was that?

I strain to hear. *A gunshot? An earthquake?* I strain to see. *A shattered window?* My heart races. Beads of sweat run down my neck to settle in a pool on my chest. I wait to hear more.

Nothing. Silence.

A nightmare?

Rolling off the foam mattress, I smack my head on the Formica headboard and stumble sideways against the wall. I flip on the light to see the front door wide open and a man in overalls walking through my living room.

What should I do?

I could see the *Guardian* headline racing through my brain: LONDON WOMAN RAPED AND MURDERED IN MUMBAI FLAT.

A plane swoops low overhead, throttling back for a landing. A train whistle cries out in the distance. Rain splatters against the windows. The cool stone floor prickles the soles of my feet and the oily smell of Brylcreem permeates the room. I wipe my nose on the back of my hand and push the hair off my forehead. I feel my pulse beating, my head throbbing. The man twenty feet from me looks around the room. Skinny and not much taller than I – around one metre-seventy – he's strong enough to overpower, rape or even strangle me. His bushy eyebrows join together at the bridge of his nose like one long, hairy caterpillar. He holds something in his right hand, but I can't quite make out what.

A gun? A knife? Am I his intended victim?

When he sees me, he freezes, eyes bulging as if he's come face to face with a villain from *Star Trek*. Or perhaps he's never seen a white woman wearing only knickers and a tank top before.

My options flash by. *Run back into the bedroom and dive beneath the bed! Collapse onto my knees and beg for mercy! Or what?*

My breathing is too loud, too heavy. I pant as if I've just run up six flights of stairs. The walls close in and the light flickers and dims. And I stand, paralysed.

The train rumbles closer. The whistle blows again, shrill and menacing; the *clickety-clack* slows. A scream cries out from nowhere.

'*Go!*' I shout. '*Go, go, go!*' I sound like a witch cursing an evil spirit. Now it's the man who stands frozen, staring at me as I charge him, waving my arms and shrieking before punching his hands. Whatever he's holding falls to the floor. The sound echoes like a bomb as he turns, recoils and sprints barefoot for the door.

The security chain, a weak protector, lies on the ground like a decapitated snake. I kick it aside, along with a pile of newspapers and slam the door shut. I push a chair and the coffee table against the entrance, barricading myself in. For the moment I feel safer. Forehead throbbing, I sink into a chair. And breathe. Once more.

I look out the window at the early morning sky – grey and polluted with city lights and smoke. It's only five o'clock and my score on the Holmes and Rahe stress scale – recent widowhood, changing jobs, and moving to another universe – surges. I'm not only alone and far from home, but also in danger. *Physical* danger. I gave up everything I had left for what? For *this*? *Something's got to give.*

* * *

Earlier that day, I met with Mohan, the HR manager, to finalise my accommodation. He gave me a Blackberry, a laptop, a security tag and an office and told me Khamat would be my driver for as long as I was there.

'We've rented you a flat in a block that is popular with expats,' he said, tapping on his phone and holding it out to me to show a photo. 'See? I wish I could live there too. It's a new building. It took me so much time to find it.'

'Well, thank you,' I said, even though I would have preferred making friends with locals rather than foreigners. 'I can't tell you how much I appreciate your help.' I shook his hand and went along with the flow. After all, the company was paying for this corporate flat. And I knew little about the neighbourhoods and travel times.

'It's a very nice place,' he said. 'The security is good. Very modern, with two bedrooms, two bathrooms and cleaning and maintenance services.' He tapped his fingers on his desk as if playing a piano.

'Sounds wonderful,' I said. It looked better than I'd expected. Still, I was anxious to see it in person and settle in.

That afternoon flew by as Mohan paraded an endless stream of forms before me to sign. By the time I'd taken a tour of the office, and met managers, secretaries, and the ever-important IT team, I was exhausted and looking forward to putting up my feet and relaxing in my new home.

Khamat picked me up and we set off to the block of flats. 'How far is it?' I asked, looking around at the gridlock.

'Not far,' Khamat said, shifting gears and scowling at the grinding sound from the transmission. 'Only ten ks.'

'Any back streets we can take?'

I soon learned that, as much as I tried to avoid it, the topic of traffic jams was how I would start and end my days from then on. In time, I'd learn not to ask how far away some place was but, rather, how long it would take to get there. In Mumbai, distance is meted out in hours and minutes, not in kilometres.

'No, *merrim*,' Khamat said. 'There are no detours. We are needing to stick to the main road. It is always taking some time. The traffic tonight is much terrible.' He raised his hands to heaven as if to apologise for his own sins. 'Only from eleven o'clock at night when changing the shifts at the call centres is finishing, until maybe seven-thirty in the morning. Now I don't know what is happening. Too much gridlock.'

Khamat turned toward me, arching his back. 'Please, *merrim*,' he said, his voice stronger and louder. 'No detours.

The side streets are going around in circles. We are needing to stick to the main road.' He let go of the steering wheel, allowing his hands to sink to his lap. Jet-lagged, tired and grumpy, I closed my eyes and tried to relax. My lower back ached and my neck stiffened as the car lurched forward again.

The road leading to my apartment building passed through a slum. Kids sat cross-legged at the edge of the pavement, some chatting and others curled up under a tarpaulin. Fully dressed men dozed everywhere or leaned against the tin walls of the shacks. Some toiled away in their dim worksheds, sanding furniture, repairing rusty bicycles, ironing clothes or weaving marigolds into garlands. Men's shirts, once white but now grey and grimy, hung on poles to air out. At least the monsoon's deluge had stopped. *What do they do when the gutters clog up and the roads flood?*

As hard as I tried, I couldn't imagine how awful it was to live in those flimsy huts. Held together by duct tape and rope, they sprouted from the pavement one after another like so many rusting mushrooms. Papers, rags and plastic bags littered the narrow walkways. Starving dogs and feral cats with matted coats loomed everywhere. I asked Khamat about the neighbourhood.

'This peoples in this suburb called Tardeo are very much poor,' Khamat said. 'You see, for everyone there is only one toilet block with one tap. Inside it is very stinking, very bad. Sometimes the water is only trickling. Also, it is not tasting good.'

The car slowed before coming to a stop. A woman beside us bent down toward a tap, raised a pink plastic tub onto her head, and walked across the road – her damp floral sari clinging to her shoulders, back, and thighs. I gave a quick thanks for my privilege as we continued on our journey to a modern complex surrounded by high walls capped with barbed wire. An iron security gate held up a marble arch on top of two towering Doric columns. The gate slid open to reveal a courtyard the size of a football pitch.

Inside, a guard, whose name I never did learn, escorted me to my new flat on the eighth floor. Even though it was close to midnight, he strode along confidently, as if he'd only recently come on duty, carting one large suitcase in each of his muscular hands.

'Welcome, *merrim,*' he said, opening the front door. 'Be happy here, please.'

He handed me a key and, like an army major standing at attention, stroked his moustache as I smiled and walked in. 'Welcome,' he said again, clicking his heels together, 'enjoy your stay very much.'

'*Shukriya*, thank you.' I nodded. I watched him leave and then locked the door. And made sure to slip on the security chain.

Inside I breathed in the newness. I turned and quickly scanned the room. It was spacious enough, decorated with a glass coffee table, a black imitation leather sofa and a matching armchair.

Even though my eyes felt heavy, I couldn't resist unpacking my blouses, trousers and jackets, and the few framed family photos I'd brought along with me from London. I picked up the one of John standing with me on London Bridge, pressed my lips against the glass, and paused for several seconds.

'A new start in a new home and you're here with me,' I whispered.

After taking a closer look around, I unpacked one of my suitcases and began arranging my toiletries in the bathroom. I brushed my teeth and washed and moisturised my face. Slipping into a T-shirt, I offered a silent prayer of gratitude. At least I was dry and comfortable and not living in the gutter.

I learned quickly enough that my flat overlooked a railway crossing. Every few minutes, a high-pitched whistle cried out just before the raucous horns announced the arrival of the trains clacking by. Cars hooted. Sirens screamed. And my gratitude quickly turned to irritation.

Oh, just get on with it, will you? Compared to most people, you've got a life of luxury.

I slid the balcony door shut to seal out the racket until I heard the click of the lock. Switching on the bedroom air-conditioner, I flopped down on the bed as the machine grunted and groaned like a patient on life support. If this was my new life, I wondered if I'd be able to handle it. I didn't wonder long. Within minutes, I was sound asleep.

I couldn't say how long I'd been dozing before it happened. That loud *bang*. Scary.

It had become my nature to be resilient and take things in stride. All through John's illness, I stayed strong. For *him*. Along the way, I'd encountered so much emotional turmoil to deal with. *Dead from the neck down. Shut down all feelings. Jump over hurdles.* Wash, rinse, repeat.

It's my way of coping. The only way I have of getting through every hour of every day. After John died, I started to believe that I was strong enough to deal with anything.

Now, as the sky turns from grey to navy, I open the flat's balcony door and watch the booms at the railway crossing lift and lower. I reflect on the night's break-in, and see again the man breaking into the living room. I know I can't stay here another day. I can't live in a home where I don't feel safe. It's a deal-breaker. *So, that's it. I'm leaving. Leaving my flat and maybe I'll even have to leave Mumbai.*

It won't be easy now, admitting I was wrong when I walked into a new life I deliberately chose for myself. But better to be wrong than to be scared. I get ready to jump in the shower before packing up my clothes, toiletries and photographs. *And then, I'm out of here.*

But I'm wrong again. I take off my T-shirt and slip into the cubicle before turning on the tap. Nothing happens. There's no water. Not from the shower head, not from the taps at the basin. I pull on a damp sweatshirt, knickers and a pair of trousers and shift the furniture away from the front door. In the hall, the first rays of sunlight filter into the small foyer, lighting my way. I lock the front door behind me and look around, unsure of where to turn first. Suddenly, a middle-aged man with curly blond hair turns down the corridor toward me.

'Hello!' I call out, waving at him. 'Excuse me!' I hurry up to him before he has a chance to escape. He looks around to see if I'm calling to someone else.

'Excuse me,' I say again, 'I don't mean to impose, but I need some help. I just moved into my flat last night, and I don't seem to have any water.' I stop and sigh, trying to slow down and look a little helpless – but not *too* helpless. 'And I was wondering…is there someone I need to call? A caretaker or superintendent or someone who can help?'

'Oh, well…welcome, neighbour.' He extends his hand, warm and dry. 'Unfortunately, it isn't all that uncommon not to have water here,' he adds. He smiles and shrugs, slipping his hands into the pockets of his khakis.

'Oh, no. I was just going to shower before work.'

'Well, I always keep a few extra buckets in my flat. I can give you one if you'd like.'

I feel my face fall, and he notices it, too.

'Or,' he continues, 'you can just wait until the problem is fixed. It usually doesn't last more than a couple of hours.'

'Oh, no. Please. I'd be very grateful for some water…if you're sure it's not too much trouble.'

I follow him to his flat and wait outside for him to bring a bucket out. After carting it over to my place, I undress and step into the shower. Using a plastic jug, I quickly soap my body, and shampoo and rinse my hair before stepping out and drying off. I slip into a black pantsuit with a white blouse, smelling of lavender soap.

First no security. Then no water.

I finish stuffing my belongings into two suitcases and stumble out into the corridor, dragging my bags behind me. When the lift arrives, I step in and collapse against the back wall.

This is not for me. Uh-uh. *Not me. Enough is enough. One thing after another. One threat after another. I can't take this.*

I tell the guard at reception that I'll be leaving the flat. For *good.* He shakes his head and mumbles, 'So sorry, *merrim.'* I hand him my key, and he shrugs. Khamat, who must've been watching the entrance, pulls the car up and stops. He frowns when he sees the bags. I ask him how he's doing.

'I'm sleeping very good in the car, *merrim*,' he replies, 'thank you. And you?' He hesitates and cocks his head to one side. 'You okay?'

Nodding, I try to smile but I'm too tired to go through the entire story. How can I possibly explain?

'Please can we keep my bags in the boot?' I say, shaking my head. Khamat frowns. I press on. 'I can't stay here another night. It's not safe for me.'

He closes the door and slips in behind the wheel before throwing the car in gear and pulling out into traffic.

Toward what? I wonder. *Certainly not toward what I had imagined.*

By the time we reach corporate headquarters over an hour later, I'm slumped back in the seat, head lolling to one side, struggling to keep my eyes open. I take the elevator to my boss's floor and peek into his cabin, the local word for office, before knocking. He stands up from behind his desk, motions me in, and clasps me by my shoulder. 'Well, well. So…good to see you again. Did you sleep well last night?' He takes a short step back as he looks me over. 'You're looking very tired. What are those black rings under your eyes? Let's hope you're not getting sick like so many other visitors. Do you feel alright?'

I pause, take a deep breath, and explain about the noise that awoke me before dawn. Someone breaking in. Smashing the security chain. That's all I could think of. I tell him I just don't feel safe there, and I can't live in a flat where I don't feel safe.

'Of course. I understand.'

I'm taken aback at his response – almost as if he'd been expecting me to complain. I take another breath. 'Would it be possible to…find other accommodation?' I bite the inside of my cheek, waiting for him to tell me it would be best that I leave India and return to London. What else *can* he say?

'Of course. So, we must find you a good place, yes? And I'm so sorry for your experience.' He looks down at his Blackberry, dials a number, and talks into the phone in Hindi, a language I don't understand. He clicks off and turns to me.

'That was my estate agent. He's going to call you so that you can work together to find a more suitable home. Something safer.'

One less thing to worry about.

He motions me to sit, and I settle into a chair opposite him as he calls his secretary to get the *coffeewalla* to bring us drinks. I feel a second wind coming, a burst of energy, and I sit taller. I'm surprised at the extent to which he's going to make me feel comfortable. I can't help but wonder what kind of gracious consideration a UK employer would show his new Indian executive if the situation were reversed.

'In the meantime,' Rama says, 'you will stay safe and comfortable at the Marine Hotel until you get settled.' He turns to his laptop. 'Now that we've got that sorted out, let's make sure everything else goes smoothly.'

He presses the keypad on his Blackberry. 'Mohan, can you come over here for a few minutes?' He nods and smiles at me. 'Yes, please. We need to get Susan settled in.'

I feel better. *Much* better. And I feel better still when I finally learn the truth about my invader – the guy who broke in earlier that morning. A member of the housekeeping staff, he was no doubt terrified out of his wits at the scantily dressed, shrieking foreigner who screamed at him. He'd been instructed to put newspapers in the living rooms of all the flats. That's what I saw in his hand and thought it was a gun. But why force the security latch? And why so early? I never do get satisfactory answers.

But I do know one thing. I'm just going to have to make it through another day. And many more nights.

Because, apparently, I'm here to stay.

CHAPTER 6

Lost

In Bandra, my neighbourhood Mumbai market, an enclave of hundreds of small shops lies hemmed into one-way alleys with no pavements. Cars dodge pedestrians, bicycles, motorbikes and swaying tuk-tuks overloaded with passengers or laden with bags of mangoes, coconuts and cooking oil.

When I walk there on Sundays, I watch that I don't step into cow pats or get rammed by a biker. I'm careful that I don't trip over a beggar, step on a banana skin in the gutter or walk into a live electric wire hanging too low for safety. My breath quickens when I enter a small Aladdin's cave – a shack filled with ribbons and silks, braids and buttons that make Selfridges' haberdashery department look puny. I try on kitschy drop earrings with silver tassels and buy gold hair clips to tame my unruly shoulder-length tresses. Everything and anything is available from these tiny shops: tampons, antibiotics and Cadbury's chocolates. If the owner doesn't have what I want, he sprints down the lane and returns a few minutes later with the perfect purse, pen or notebook.

In this market you can find tailors, barber shops, hair salons, and car-sized stores selling shampoo, deodorants, nail polish, aloe vera creams and magic lotions to make your face whiter and younger-looking. Guavas, watermelons, potatoes, carrots, fragrant celery and garlic and red and yellow chillies swell the wooden carts, their axles straining beneath the loads. Chickens cackle in their cages. I choose one, and it squawks at me as the butcher lifts it out. I don't see him twisting its neck and chopping off its head. A few minutes later it's de-feathered, cleaned, chopped into quarters, wrapped in newspaper and stuffed in my shopping basket – still warm.

For most of us, being jostled at close quarters is suffocating and scary, but in that benign hubbub my senses come alive. Aromas of cinnamon and cumin complement sights of scarlet saris and glitzy bangles. The kaleidoscope of shops selling bales of organza and hand-embroidered cotton amid the constant blaring of Bollywood songs makes me want to shimmy and tap my toes. I no longer feel as if I'm a condemned prisoner in a jail cell I'd built around me. Now, sunlight streams through the barred window, and I feel I might soon free myself, if only on parole.

Along these backstreets, squalor and glamour coexist. Behind darkened car windows, chauffeurs drive Shah Rukh Khan, Amitabh Bachchan and other Bollywood celebs, wearing Gucci sunglasses, in air-conditioned limousines past families living on the sweltering pavements. Past the beggar with stumps for arms, sunken cheeks and protruding ribs. Past the mothers draped in violet and polyester saris hunched over small fires made of twigs and rubbish, preparing their one daily meal of rice and lentils. Past the hungry kids who need no encouragement to eat, wolfing down their lunch from a piece of filthy newspaper. Past the poverty they don't see.

One steamy evening on the way home from work, Khamat drives me through the labyrinth of narrow lanes to the tailor to pick up my new shalwar kameez. Pedestrians thump on the car bonnet to make sure we don't bump into them. Our wheels graze stacks of mangoes and baskets of tomatoes. Sulphurous smog stings my eyes. The car door misses a wall by centimetres. I realise that gasping as we navigate yet another precarious corner is an irrational reaction, but at least it makes me feel momentarily thinner. I wish I could say the same for our car.

A cyclist stops to restack cartons of eggs half a metre high on the small carrier on the back of his bike and then eases back into the saddle and somehow, balancing his fragile load, pedals away. We inch forward, amidst honking and yelling, careful not to bump into a dawdling cow munching on coriander leaves.

The criss-cross latticed lanes narrow, and the flow of people, bikes and rickshaws stops.

'Where do we go now?' Khamat asks.

I don't know, and I know he *knows* I don't know.

Khamat shifts in his seat and turns his head to look at me. 'Left or right, *merrim?*'

I rub my forehead and stare at the gridlock ahead of us. A stranger in the rearview mirror gawks back at me. I don't recognise the tangerine kurta or loose shirt, the long gold drop earrings or my shoulder-length hair. What has happened to the short business bob? Yes, I've managed to shove the grieving widow who used to wear those white or black button-up blouses with black pants to the back of my wardrobe. She no longer exists.

Change is working on the outside, but my insides remain painfully confused as I flounder in my own personal no-man's land of my own making. I smile cynically at the reflection of myself. This search for a new me straddling a world without my John is more complicated than I could have imagined.

Well-meaning friends and family gave advice as to how to rebuild my life. Meet someone. Socialise. Remarry. Easy. But nothing worked. Maybe I wasn't ready, or maybe I have to do it my way. During first dates introduced by colleagues and friends, all I saw were the shiny bald heads, potbellies, prickly moustaches and tufts of hair sprouting out of oversized ears. Stories about ex-wives, high cholesterol, how much money they'd won gambling in Macau or Monaco, or cruising down the Volga bored me. Not only had my inner compass lost direction, but I couldn't even find my way around my own neighbourhood.

'Let me just drive round a bit and we will find that tailor,' Khamat says, filling my silence. When the traffic moves, he wipes his forehead with a white handkerchief, puts the car into first gear and we trundle on.

The miniscule stores in the market all look the same. Rolls of red, silver and magenta silks lean towards us between branches of bananas. The pungent smell of garlic and onions, of curry leaves and ginger tickle my nose. The aroma of sweet mangoes disappears around a corner into a quick jab of ammonia from a nearby public toilet.

I'm just about to give up any hope of finding the tailor when I spot him hunched over his treadle Singer machine on the side of the road. His eyes are glued to the needle as he gently slides lime-green fabric beneath the presser foot. His bare feet bounce up and down on the treadle, oblivious of the traffic. Wheels and feet miss his toes by inches.

'Here, that's him,' I shout. 'That's Hitesh, the tailor!'

Khamat punches the brakes and, as the car slows, I throw open the door and squeeze out. I call to the man. Hitesh remembers me and the trousers. The only 'foreigner' in the neighbourhood, I'm difficult to forget. I stand out. When people can't pronounce my name, I call myself *Sushma*, an easy word to remember. It means the beautiful girl next door. Is Sushma now becoming the *real* me?

Hitesh rummages through a pile of clothes on a table in the back as if he's a retriever on the scent of a wounded duck. He straightens his back and looks down, bewildered. Khamat drives around the block again and again. I swat a fly away from my face and crouch inside to help. There's no sign of my outfit and I close my eyes and grimace.

'Don't worry, *merrim*,' Hitesh grins, 'they are here somewhere. I make them short only this morning.'

Hitesh's thick eyebrows hover over bloodshot eyes as he stares at the pile of clothes around him. Lying under a stool on the floor, a baby with bright-pink ribbons in her hair smiles and stretches out her tiny hand to touch me. Somehow, there's always a sparkle of joy in the most unexpected places. I tickle the girl's arm, and she giggles as if she's a princess lying on a goose-down pillow. Her eyes are full of the best kinds of mischief.

My moods yo-yo up and plummet down. A smile, sensing joy or energy from a stranger, swells my heart with hope, at least for a while. Looking at that laughing baby, I breathe in the courage to carry on. If she can smile lying on a slab of concrete under her grandfather's worktable then I can laugh at the sight of the tailor – and me after joining him – scratching around his shop floor on our hands and knees.

A miracle worker, Hitesh lifts up the crumpled pair of loose-fitting pantaloons and the matching shirt and shakes off the dust and whatever else is on them. Bits of fabric and thread fly off into the evening air.

'There! You see,' he says, a smile widening on his face. 'You must stop to worry so much. It will always be all right in the end.'

I'm only beginning to master how everything will be 'all right'. How far is it to the 'end' anyway?

Hitesh smiles wider; his lips and teeth, reddish-brown from chewing on betel nuts, betray his delight. He sprays water over the garments and picks up an old-fashioned iron, filled with smouldering coals, and strokes the fabric. The loud hissing sound smothers the honking and shouting only feet away. Steam clouds up. Droplets fall on my glasses, blurring my vision. Will I *ever* be able to see where I'm going?

Hitesh wraps the pressed trousers and shirt in newspaper, ties the package with string, and finishes it off with a bow as if we were in Harrods. Just then, Khamat rounds the corner again and, as he slows down, I open the door and hop in the moving vehicle, before we set off for the drive home.

Soon, a glittering vermillion BMW, washed and polished, drives right toward us, and Khamat brakes again. People yell at the BMW driver that he's going the wrong way, but he doesn't seem to hear. Bikes, cars and pedestrians – and even a rambling cow – all grind to a halt. Horn blasts grow louder, a tribute to Tchaikovsky's *1812 Overture*. People shove against one another.

Pandemonium – there's nowhere to go.

Suddenly, the passenger-side door of the BMW swings open and a plump woman wearing an emerald sari and white patent, high-heeled sandals jumps out, leaving her driver inside. She begins waving her arms and shouting like a cop. Ignoring the one-way road sign, she waddles towards the stalled traffic, waving two flabby arms, yelling at everyone to reverse. Her pony tail waves defiantly behind her. Crimson fingernails wag in the faces of disobedient citizens. In her impromptu role, she seems to enjoy every minute of her new position. I envy her knowing what she wants and how to get it. Nothing's going to hold *her* back.

'Back, back!' she shrieks, waving at the traffic behind us.

Subjects of the realm, everyone obeys. Rickshaws and cars begin rolling in the wrong direction. People stumble after them. Khamat grinds the gears into reverse and follows her orders, negotiating between potholes and baskets of onions.

The woman, back in her BMW, rolls down her window as the car drives past.

'So sorry, madam, and thank you,' she shouts at me, leaving us in a cloud of dust.

'You're welcome,' I yell back. I feel my lips curl into a smile. I wonder if John is up there somewhere, revelling right along with me at the woman's audacity. As irritated as I feel over being held up for half an hour, I harbour a grudging admiration for her ability to take control of an absurd situation and make everyone do her bidding. *And* pull it off.

Can I, too, learn to take control of my life one day?

A screech of metal against metal slices the din. Over my shoulder, I see the BMW stalled in its tracks. Steam rises from its engine. A few seconds later, Khamat opens his door and steps out into the street to join the cheering and whistling crowds. A woman carrying a baby in her arms throws her silver-striped dupatta into the air and ululates, whirling around like a Bollywood dervish.

'See, *merrim*,' Khamat calls to me, pointing. 'They got her after all. She won't come driving here in her expensive car again, shouting at us to go backwards! See her car now.' He punches his fist on the hooter as if he were slapping a bongo drum.

People clamour around the vehicle to inspect the damage. The woman jumps out of the car, unleashing a tirade of obscenities that even I understand.

I settle back in my seat again and think, maybe it's best, after all, not to be *quite* so bossy. And maybe trying to take control of everyone isn't *quite* the right way to go about doing things. Finding my own inner sparkle again will take time. It's not as easy as the woman appeared to make it seem. The tailor was right, I think. It's not worthwhile worrying so much. I just have to keep moving forward, following, not pushing against the flow.

Sitting in the car, waiting for things to calm down and Khamat to start us moving again, I hug my new outfit to my chest.

I can't wait to wear it.

CHAPTER 7

Just a Painting

That painting is me.

In the main hall of the Museum of Modern Art in Mumbai, I stand in front of an oil painting of two black women, with painted lips and eyebrows, facing but not looking at one another. Their subdued eyes stare out in the distance. Strength flows from their firm arms and down their rigid backs.

Lost in their intimacy, I see myself sitting there with them, squatting on a prickly, tiger-striped straw mat, waiting for a signal. Stepping closer I can feel their arms embracing me as if they're pulling me into their world. Ceiling fans whir overhead, struggling to shift the heavy, humid air. The breeze urges my floral kurta to ripple against my back.

I'm mesmerised.

Extraordinary, how that painting captures my melancholy. My loss. Twisting my wedding ring with the thumb and forefinger of my right hand, I take a step closer.

The painting's colours – ghee, saffron, pineapple, turmeric, honey, mango – reach out to me as if to remind me that I, too, was once all those delicious shades. Before my John had been diagnosed with terminal cancer. Before asbestos fibres sucked the life out of his lungs. Before he took his last breath. When his body stiffened, I turned sage grey. Like the herb's leaves – slightly sour, bitter and rough to the touch. My unique warm glow-sunflower-yellow stifled.

'I'm sorry for your loss,' friends and colleagues repeated for weeks after John died in our London home.

What did that mean? My loss? It's true. I lost things. My credit card, the lapis necklace John had bought me for my birthday, hope and light. But I hadn't lost John.

He was always there.

Waiting, watching, whispering.

In the dingy wintery mornings after John died, I heard him singing in the shower, 'I'll be loving you always'. Over breakfast, his large hand fondled my petite fingers. When I left for work I tasted his lips on mine for hours afterward. Our mattress smelled of his musky scent and I missed his gentle snoring.

But he'd been gone for months.

Something needed to change, but I wasn't willing to let go of his diaries, his ties, his toothbrush. All I could think of was how my desperate struggle to keep him alive had failed. And how all the colour in my life had faded.

One steamy Sunday afternoon, I leave my Mumbai flat to explore the city. The heat radiates off the pavement and the sun roasts my back. Buses belch black fumes as they butt their way through traffic. Bodies bump into me in the overcrowded streets. It feels strange that I'm not bothered by the chaotic infringement. Noise and movement are exactly what I need. The intense contrasting smells of sugary bananas, sweating bodies and public toilets reeking of ammonia remind me that I'm alive. *Still.*

A hawker badgers me to buy a fresh coconut. He chops off the top of its rounded head with a machete and sticks a straw into the juice. The pure, refreshing liquid moistens my parched throat.

It's then that I see a banner hanging limply on the walls of a large domed building: SPECIAL EXHIBITION FOR LOCAL ARTISTS – TODAY ONLY. I wander into the museum's sprawling atrium where shafts of light slice through the windows of the expansive hall. In the strong sunlight, beige particles of dust dance on the whitewashed walls. I stroll from painting to painting until I stop, riveted.

In front of the one that's me.

For a while, I see nothing except the confused expressions on the two women's faces. I don't hear the chatter of groups of visitors, nor the giggles of two young girls running round in circles. I don't smell the aroma of vegetable samosas or pay attention to the others shuffling past me in the crowded auditorium. I close my eyes and try to steady myself.

Never before has one work of art affected me in this way. Someone I've never met has captured my hidden feelings with the sweep of a brush and a few tubes of paint. To the outside world, I may appear vibrant, even courageous, but deep inside, like the black shading in the painting, my mood is heavy.

Without thinking, I run my finger through my wavy hair to see if I too can twist my curls like theirs into a knot at the back of my neck. But my hair is too short. Prickly strands poke into the palm of my hand, while theirs, lightly oiled, cling to the back of their necks. My baggy cotton salwar kameez hangs limply down to my knees. Theirs – lemon-yellow, soft and silky – drapes softly over full breasts, revealing slender midriffs.

Those two women, like me, are looking for a way out of that dark background. No wonder this painting speaks to me. For the very first time, at the age of sixty, I have no clue who I am. Yet as I marvel at their alluring outfits, I recognise that I'm beginning to try to change. When I look in the mirror in the mornings, I see olive-green eyeliner, thick mascara, long drop earrings and a little too much blush. Bouncy waves replace the flat-ironed layered business bob. Changes that for now seem cosmetic. If I start with my appearance, I keep hoping that my spirit will wiggle its way back into my crumpled soul.

In the museum's bright hall, I cover my mouth with the palm of my left hand and gaze at the painting with the women's gold thong sandals, shiny anklets and glinting toe rings. Bangles, the tint of a harvest moon, cover their arms. From their lips and eyebrows, glowing brassy tones peek out from the shadows urging me to laugh again. But thick eyeliner shrouds their maudlin eyes, revealing signs of lethargy.

My inside light, like theirs, has run out of power. But now I'm trying to find the switch.

Strangely enough, it's in India – where initially I have no friends, no family and no social life – that I finally begin to sleep through the night again. My daily yoga asanas in a large hall where women lie down on cloth mats doing their own self-practice begins to ease me out of a deep sleep.

As I balance on one leg in 'tree pose', the deafening noise from the street below dissipates. The constant blaring and rumblings from the gridlocked traffic, the grumbling of low-flying planes and the crows' jarring calls fade into the background. All I hear is my own breathing as my belly pumps the yogi 'breath of fire'. *In, out. In, out.* After two hours my body feels looser, my limbs lighter and my forehead relaxed. I don't feel quite so alone.

The force of collective healing.

My taste buds also summon me back to life. Plain omelettes and grilled cheese sandwiches now seem bland. It's taken a while to get used to spicy food at every meal, but now I relish tandoori chicken, vegetable Biryani, garlicky black lentils, chilli chickpeas and cauliflower fried with turmeric, curry leaves, cardamom and ginger. Cinnamon is an olfactory nirvana. I can't stop eating juicy Alphonso mangoes and golden papayas, or scooping up daal in warm chappati and licking the gravy off my fingertips.

Invitations to dine at colleagues' and neighbours' homes nurse me back into society. I feel a deep connection to my foodie hosts as if I've lived here before in this large family.

These are my musings as I – entranced by this painting in the walnut wooden frame on the white museum wall – am astonished at the resemblance to me. I feel at home here. No longer a foreigner in this strange new world, I'm trying to fathom whom I'm becoming.

Someone near me whispers, 'Do you like it?' A petite woman wearing a jade sari looks at me. The soft fabric lies across her forearm. Silver-looped earrings frame her broad cheeks. She throws her one long plait over her shoulder, and I breathe in a citrus fragrance.

'It seems to speak to me,' I reply, looking down at the stone floor, unsure what to say to the stranger.

'My name is Patti. I'm the artist,' she says. Her voice has a lilt to it as if she's chanting. Palm stretching out, she touches my elbow. 'What is your good name?'

'I'm Susan,' I say.

What a lovely custom to preface 'good', when asking a person's name. Patti clasps my right hand with both of hers. 'Would you like to buy it?' she asks, bowing her head slightly.

I take a step back. This is the last thing on my mind. Can I afford it? Where will I put it in my tiny Mumbai flat? And yet, I connect with the warmth of her hand and the tinkling of her silver bracelet. 'I see you sitting there with them,' Patti says, waving a hand over the women's faces. She turns to look at me. 'The eyes…yours and theirs…are looking the same way.'

I stop breathing. John would have loved it.

All I know is that I have to buy it. For him. For *us*.

I don't remember walking to the cash machine to draw rupees for my purchase, nor pressing a pile of notes into Patti's hand. She hugs me, stuffs the notes in her purse and lifts the painting off the wall. Citrus perfume lingers. Patti wraps her work of art in newspaper tied with string. She slides a bunch of marigolds under the knot as if it's a Picasso.

With the painting tucked beneath my armpit, I walk towards the exit, and even though I hold a heavy package my flip-flops barely touch the marble floor.

Outside the building, I'm blinded by the intense glare, but my eyes adjust quickly. A few minutes later I find myself in the back seat of a tuk-tuk, clinging to a pole and bouncing to my Mumbai home. I don't feel the need to wave away the clouds of exhaust fumes or wipe my watery eyes. All that matters is that the precious painting survives the potholes and sharp twists and turns.

Some years later, I hang the painting of those two women in a prominent position on a soft purple wall next to the front door of my Seattle home. Now, every time I unlock and lock my front door, they remind me that I'm still not sure who I am, or who I want to be. That same gloomy undercurrent tries to smother our shimmer, but the yellow hues glint brighter and lighter.

That painting is me.

FAITH

CHAPTER 8

The Making of a Merry Widow

A few weeks after I begin my new job, the chairman, Mr Rajpul, the man people revere, the man to whom people bow, and the man who few see, invites me to lunch.

'Shree Rajpul, he wants to talk to you about the new CEO he is hiring for the fertiliser division,' his personal assistant, Manoj, says. 'You are so much lucky,' Manoj mumbles into the phone. 'He hardly ever has lunch with one of his team.' He cuts me off in mid-sentence as he disconnects the call.

In corridors and cabins – as offices are called here – the chairman's name is always whispered in hushed, hallowed tones. He's addressed as *Shree*, a Sanskrit word that's a title typically reserved for veneration of the gods or famous, rich people.

The executive offices here in corporate India exude an air of international sophistication, much the same as those in London, Frankfurt and Istanbul. Personal assistants sit outside their boss's offices like bulldogs guarding a bone. Shoes swish on Persian carpets, objects d'art grace the walls and the mahogany chairs are engraved with tigers, palms and water lilies. The aroma of freshly brewed coffee fills the air. Here, ivory and granite statues stand on the yellowwood coffee tables beneath towering marble columns and chandeliers that look as though they've come from Versailles. The atmosphere is a tad more formal – no first names. More, 'yes, sir,' and less challenge to the boss.

When Shree Raipur enters the executive dining room, the diners, all members of the senior leadership team, stand up until a waiter pulls out his chair and he sits down. He nods at his team, who sit in twos and threes at other tables. Two waiters wearing crisp white shirts with black waistcoats and trousers place starched white linen napkins on our laps and hover at our table as if we're royalty. Aromas of cardamom and fennel fill the room.

'So how do you like our food?' my new boss enquires, tucking his napkin into the top of his open-neck shirt and twisting the ends of his 'handlebar' moustache.

'I love it,' I reply, tearing off a piece of warm naan and scooping up the fragrant chana masala, curried chickpeas. 'Especially the lentils and masala potatoes.'

Rajpul adjusts his collar and continues. 'And how are you settling down in your new flat now? Please let me know if there is anything you need.'

'Everything is fine so far. Thank you for asking, Shree,' I add in the reverent custom.

People in Mumbai are so warm and friendly and genuinely concerned for my welfare. My choice to resign from my London job and move temporarily to India where everything is so different begins to lift my mood. I wake to a spiritual world where shrines grace street corners, the muezzin calls devotees to prayer at sunrise, and churches fill for early morning prayers, even on weekdays.

A bustling world of teeming streets, animated chatter and incessant mobile phone ringtones; where markets expel aromas of celery, parsley, mangoes and bananas and where baskets of onions sleep side-by-side with street dwellers; where designer sunglasses, diamond-studded saris and air-conditioned chauffeur-driven limousines are close neighbours with malnourished families and children defecating in the gutters; where the ever-present holy cow ambles unperturbed. And where, in the mornings, I entertain a green parrot that sits on my balcony railing, his head cocked to the side, watching me breathe through a yoga series of sun salutations.

It's fun to wear all the wonderful colours – pinks, purples and yellows – that the Colour Me Beautiful experts said didn't suit my sallow skin tone. My old self-image – serious and sombre widowhood – is beginning to fade. At least from the outside I look and feel different.

Perhaps because John isn't with me in this new world, I see the back of his head in fewer places. I speak with him less frequently, and his kisses become less persistent. There are no restaurants, coffee shops or museums where we'd spent time together, and memories of all the good times we enjoyed, are returning. Fewer images of John losing weight, moaning in pain, and crying because he didn't want to die, haunt me.

Chairman Raipul's mobile phone rings, but he ignores it. This is a compliment. Most of the managers seem to be on their phones most of the time – even in meetings. He carefully wipes the corners of his mouth, twists the corner of his moustache again, and leans against the back of his chair, patting his stomach.

'I'm happy to hear that you're settling down well.' He

smiles. 'Sometimes foreigners find it difficult to adapt to India – our spicy food and noisy culture. And your husband, is he settling down okay?'

A waiter leans forward to fill our glasses with hot chai. Surprised that the head of HR hasn't told him that I'm a widow, I splutter on a mouthful of the fragrant tea. 'Sadly, my husband passed away last year,' I reply, feeling the spicy food bubbling in my stomach. 'So I'm here on my own.'

'You mean he's expired?' Mr Raipul raises his thin eyebrows.

Not wanting him to see the tears welling up, I nod gravely and look away. Caught off guard by the mention of the word 'husband', my throat tightens. I can't help it, especially if I'm nervous. And lunch with the chairman is unnerving.

I'd bought myself a special outfit for this first important meeting – a bright apricot-and-lime shalwar kameez – spent the whole of the previous evening preparing for our meeting, and now, pinching the naan bread between my thumb and fingers, I try not to choke. My cheeks begin to burn.

I have to pull myself together to be at my best.

'I understand you wish to talk about how we on-board fertiliser's CEO,' I say, hoping to divert the topic of conversation. 'Perhaps you could share the business challenges he faces.' My voice is steady now.

'*Mmm…*no,' the chairman answers laconically, as if he has an obligation to answer. 'Now is not the time.' He picks up his Blackberry and checks his emails.

Around us, men chatter, shoes squeak on the marble floor and I don't know what to say. The conversation between us wanes. Is it something I said or is he bothered by an important business issue? His mobile phone rings again, and this time he takes the call. I pretend to carry on eating while he speaks in Hindi, but now the raita tastes sour and sticky.

Concerned that I've botched my first meeting with the big boss, I can't think of what to say. I uncross my legs and press the soles of my sandals onto the floor. He recruited me all the way from London to coach his leadership team and now I'm trying to stop my legs from shaking.

'I'll call you back later,' Rajpul informs the caller after about five minutes. Then he checks his emails and texts.

'How old are your children, sir?' I ask, hopeful that changing the topic might help. My voice is too tentative and an octave too high.

'They are both students at Harvard now. My son is completing his MBA, and my daughter is in her first year of a medical degree.' He purses his lips, looks away from me and pushes his chair back.

I press my elbows on the table to keep steady. Clearly he's not interested in continuing our discussion. Naively, I've no idea what I've said or done to offend him.

'Was there anything you wished to discuss about our leadership workshop next week?' I enquire.

He doesn't answer. Instead, he pulls the napkin out of his shirt collar, tosses it on the table, stuffs his Blackberry into his suit pocket and stands up. The dining room is suddenly quiet. Very quiet. His chair scrapes against the cold marble floor as he moves back away from me. Trying to pretend everything is okay, even though I know it isn't, I stand up to shake his hand and thank him for his time. My palms are embarrassingly sweaty.

Waiters turn into statues and avert their eyes. No one

speaks, no one chews or scoops their vegetables with chappati, and no one sips their chai. What's happened? One minute we're having an affable conversation, and the next, the chairman stops eating. The lentils feel heavy in my stomach.

'Well, I must go now,' Rajpul says, stuffing his hands in his trouser pockets. 'I have another meeting to attend.'

He turns his back to me and strides out the room. His footsteps echo on the stone floor. Is executive life really so different in India? He barely touched his rice and sambal. Having worked alongside two other Indian chairmen as a coach prior to this job, I think I have a highish level of cultural sensitivity. Never have I experienced such dismissal. Obviously, I still have a lot to learn. But what? And who can I ask?

That evening, Sheetal, a young colleague in her late twenties, invites me to the cinema, where we luxuriate in reclining chairs while waiters serve samosas and cola. In an uncanny and troubling synchronicity with the lunchtime event, we see the movie *Water*. Set in 1939, nine-year-old child bride, Chuyia, whose elderly husband recently expired, walks down an alley in the streets of a town in northern India. Head shaven and wearing an ankle-length white robe, she stumbles over the cobblestones as her mother grips her elbow and pulls her along. Something awful is about to happen, but I struggle to follow the plot. The film is in Hindi, and there are no English subtitles.

'Where is she taking her daughter now?' I whisper to Sheetal, not wishing to disturb the quiet that suffocates the theatre.

'*Ahh*, you know,' she confides, her shoulder-length curls shimmering in the dark. 'In some parts of India, there is still a *biiig* stigma to being a widow.' She cups her mouth close to my ear. 'Nobody in the family wants to be burdened with an extra mouth to feed. Of course, here in Mumbai it's very different. We're more sophisticated. Widows are more accepted into society, and not so much ostracised. That young girl is going to be left in a brothel where other widows live.'

The child bride is deposited in an ashram with a group of older girls and wrinkled-faced women draped in coarse white saris. Like many other Hindu widows, she's doomed to spend the rest of her life rejected by society. Tears stream down the girl's cheeks as her mother hands her over to the lady of the house and walks away. Not a word, not a hug, nor touch. Chuyia is forced into prostitution to support the ashram. She remains convinced that her stay is temporary, and that her mother will come back to take her away. But she never does.

There it is. So obvious and yet I'd missed it.

Although widows in India no longer throw themselves on their dead husbands' funeral pyres, I didn't realise that they are still often ostracised from society. Widowhood is often a state of social death. Even in the higher castes, widows with no income are seen an inauspicious drain on resources. Some are sent away by their husbands' families who want to prevent them inheriting money or property.

I choke on the spicy samosa. I thought I was worldly, culturally sensitive and well read. How can I not have known that the word 'widow' still had such a strong negative association for some people in India? *Am I going to be stigmatised by my colleagues? Is the chairman uncomfortable with my marital status?*

Scared of what might happen, half-believing my career here is over, I don't really want to know the answer. All I know is that I hate ticking the box 'widow' whenever I complete a form requiring marital status. And there's been a lot of those lately. A form for an Indian work visa, a form for the UK mortgage, and another for the bank where John and I held a joint account. I press the handle to shift my recliner to sitting and lean my head on the back of the empty seat in front of me.

'Some of our older managers still feel uncomfortable working or socialising with widows,' Sheetal whispers, sensing my anguish. 'Especially the very orthodox people who've grown up in rural towns or villages. But don't worry, you'll be fine.'

Despite having lived and worked in many countries, it dawns on me I haven't prepared myself for widowhood in India. Yes, I've read about the horrors of widow-burning, sati, and now I'm shocked to learn that it's only been thirty years since the Indian government passed the Sati Prevention Act, to stop this practice – where widows either throw themselves or are dragged onto their dead husbands' funeral pyres. It's also a crime merely to be a bystander at such a brutal ceremony. Yet as late as 2000, there were reports that sati was still occurring in some of the rural villages.

How can I have been so ignorant as to cocoon myself in this high-tech business world? While widows are no longer aggressively banished from society, they often remain social outcasts, living in separate neighbourhoods and excluded from community life.

At work here, telling someone I'm a widow is sometimes a conversation stopper. To some, it's taboo. Unaware of the prejudices of others, I've been oblivious to this. Not that I can change anything about my situation. Two things come to mind. Except for close friends and family, my grief needs to stay closeted. Perhaps my visible despondency at being a widow, combined with the chairman's unease around that very concept, caused him to distance himself from me.

It's my new friend Gita, also recently widowed, who helps me to understand and accept my status in India. I met her through a friend of a London friend who emailed me. 'Please contact Gita. She runs a travel agency in India for incentive travel groups, and always accompanies the executives or sales reps. You'll have lots to talk about.'

She was right. Our friendship began as soon as I heard her voice. 'You must come to lunch at the Cricket Club,' she said. 'Tomorrow at two?' She laughed at the end of each sentence and often ended with a question. '*Aaccha* – good?'

When the receptionist at Mumbai's Cricket Club told me that phone calls and talking business aren't allowed, I drifted back to where I first met John for lunch – London's Reform Club in Pall Mall – formal, classy and colonial. No flashing of cash or credit cards. Members are expected to pay their bills discreetly.

The Cricket Club's restaurant, which overlooks an immaculate cricket field, buzzes with women wearing floral and striped silk saris and emerald and ruby necklaces that one expects to see on a maharani's neckline. Diamond rings glitter in the sunlight.

As soon as I walked in, Gita rushed forward to greet me as if we were sisters, hugging me with a kiss on both cheeks. One of her drop diamond earrings caught on the frame of my glasses.

'Goodness gracious,' she laughed as we tried to untangle ourselves. I couldn't stop smiling.

As soon as I sipped the mulligatawny soup made with vegetables, lentils, turmeric and tamarind, my palate tingled. Kulfi ice cream made with condensed milk gave me goose pimples. It was so good, I forgot about all the calories in each spoonful.

That was my introduction to Gita and her vibrant personality. Within seconds I knew we'd get along. We've been close friends ever since.

'Listen,' Gita said, flicking her hair behind her ears, 'next weekend I have to fly to Indore to meet with the CEO of a mobile phone company who wants to gift his top salespeople a trip to Switzerland.' I nibbled on a dried fig, not expecting her to invite me to join her. 'The town is a centre for handloom weaving in India. You'll love the kurtas and saris that they make for Gucci and Harrods. You must come with me. We can stay in a fort built in the 1500s that has been renovated into a gorgeous hotel.' I leaned forward, almost knocking over a cup of chai.

'Thanks, that would be wonderful,' I said as the corners of my mouth curled up. 'Is there anything I can do to help?'

'I can get Air India to comp us tickets,' she added, nibbling on a chocolate covered date. 'I'll let you know the flight details next week.'

A week has passed, and now, wearing garlands of marigolds, we find ourselves floating down the Saraswati River on a barge, accompanied by trumpeting conches and clanging symbols. My history lesson on widowhood continues when Gita points out small stone figurines on the paved riverbanks. Some, engraved with a foot or hand, remain huddled together at the very place where sati had occurred. We disembark and squat on the ground, offering prayers for the women burned alive on the pyres. I can almost hear their screams.

'We're lucky to be living in these progressive times.' Gita nods and takes my hand, sensing my dismay as I stare at the memorials to the burnt widows. 'We're both financially independent.' She radiates confidence, adding, 'Look at me. I run my own travel business and my brother – he works for me. I pay him a salary. And my nephew also.'

She bends over and points at another figure.

'This small statue are the husband and his faithful wife, who was burned with him.' Gita takes my hand. Her eyes are moist. 'But you know, wallowing in the past doesn't bring them back. So let's now go and get a body massage. They use sandalwood oil in this part of the country, which will banish all your worries.'

If I had any doubts about Gita's enthusiasm, they disappeared following an hour of soothing deep-tissue massage. After the treatment, Gita leads me behind several small stores where local women sit cross-legged on carpets in front of wooden looms as tall as a door frame and as thin as a broom handle, following intricate patterns to produce their fabric. There are sounds of clacking as hands run the spindles back and forth, weaving warps of cotton yarn interspersed with wefts of silk thread, carrying me back to time immemorial.

I'm fascinated to watch women spin and dye silk and cotton yarn into magnificent creations. The finished fabric, a riot of colour, glows with a silken sheen embellished with border designs inspired by local motifs and architecture. Who could resist buying scarves, pashminas, kurtas and saris? Not us! A few hours later, we find ourselves staggering under the load of our purchases back to the hotel.

'Maybe there are still some backward people who see us widows as an unwanted burden.' Gita waves her arms in the air and shimmies as we parade around the room in our new outfits. She drapes a silver- and magenta-striped pashmina over my shoulders. 'But we've shown them that we're independent, intelligent and beautiful.' She raises her arms above her head, twirling her wrists and fingers.

Could I possibly become all of those things? I lift my head and shut my eyes for a brief moment. It is as if by seeing my own fear and prejudices mirrored on such a large cultural scale, I'm finally able to begin to accept myself for who I am. Gita helps me shift into a brighter space.

'And we laugh a lot,' I add as we fold our purchases and struggle to pack everything into our small suitcases.

Gita lets out a grunt as she sits on my bag while I try to close the zip. We giggle like two teenagers.

When we board the plane back to Mumbai, heaving our bulging totes and plastic bags on our shoulders, I hum the few chants I memorised from the priests on the banks of the river.

Gita joins in, leans over and whispers, 'We believe the soul has many, many lives ahead and many experiences to undergo. You too can be happy again.'

I begin to believe that my spirit will be reborn. My own persistent joie de vivre, suppressed by mourning sickness, is beginning to push its way back into my life. On that trip I make up my mind that being a widow, especially in India, is just one of those things I need to come to terms with. I also vow not to be an emotional or financial burden to my children.

When I get back to my Mumbai home, I fold all my black-and-white blouses and skirts and stuff them into a plastic bag.

I swear never to wear these mourning colours again. *But will I be able to keep this promise when I leave India?*

CHAPTER 9

The Power of Salt and Water

Mumbai's benign hullabaloo rests on a panoply of multi-faith spirituality. Gods, temples, mosques, synagogues and churches pop up in unexpected places. Statues of Shiva, Buddha and Jesus nestle under windowsills, in rubbish-littered alleys, and in between bunches of bananas on street corners.

The muezzin call to prayer echoes across the city just before sunrise. Copper bells ring in temples and the churches fill with congregants. Auspicious dates in the Hindu calendar determine when couples may marry and when wives should fast to keep their husbands healthy.

Some CEOs consult with astrologists as well as management gurus when making strategic business decisions. They pay close attention to advice from mystics as to when or whether to make an acquisition, expand in a new geography or promote someone to a senior leadership role. Logic and mysticism blend comfortably with mobile phones, automated AI factories, a pilgrimage to the Ganges and the ever-present holy cow. An atheist, I too am captivated by this intensity of belief, gods and prayer.

Intuitively, I flow into this multi-faith culture, relishing the sincerity and beauty of office prayers. When I light the wicks embedded in the holders of the copper 'candle of learning' at the beginning of a workshop, tears fill my eyes.

On the Hindu festival Dahi Handi, I hold my breath when barefoot young men scramble to form human pyramids up to ten men high in the monsoon deluge. Flocks of goats clog the main roads during El Eid.

On Ganesh Chaturthi, a holiday celebrating the birth of Lord Ganesh, I join the procession, dancing down the street with my neighbours around a life-size statue of the elephant god. He sits in lotus pose on an elevated platform en route to the sea. In Varanasi, the holy city on the Ganges, I join the chanting priests waving lanterns against the evening sky. The imam at the Pushkar mosque blesses me as he places his palm on my turquoise hijab.

At the Yom Kippur service in the blue-domed Magen David Synagogue, I hope that familiar chants will restore my former vitality. But in my own temple, I stare at the cantor standing on the pulpit, known as a *bimah,* surrounded by an ornately carved marble and an elongated stained-glass arch that reaches the ceiling. I sit in the women's gallery upstairs, in a sea of saris, unable to connect with God, feeling nothing except inspiration for the architectural beauty.

Can I, even without praying, find an inner calmness that believers find in religion?

As if from nowhere, Aristotle's wisdom, 'knowing yourself is the beginning of all wisdom' encourages me to explore this subconscious inner journey. At sunrise, my yoga practice gets me out of bed. Fast becoming a yoga devotee, I practice different breathing techniques as well as asanas or postures, to focus on the psycho-spiritual centres of my body. I practice 'breath of fire' and 'alternate nostril breathing' to cleanse my toxins and flush out my sinuses with a nasal neti pot filled with salt water. But I want more.

A week of silent meditation in an ashram fills me with dread, although my neighbour, Sumi, swears by the experience.

'I come back a different person,' she says. 'Much more calm, attentive, and now I have no more stomach cramps. And I have lots more energy.'

The thought of not speaking or being spoken to for a week scares me. I can't keep quiet for that long. I'll go crazy by lunch, jittery by dinner and mumbling to myself like a lunatic by breakfast. Starved for answers, I search for a one-day healing meditation.

'I know exactly what you need…guaranteed to heal you, ma'am,' my secretary, Asifa, says. 'You will find your aura and then be healthy.' Her walnut eyes seem to soften. 'You know my pa, when his papa died, he was *verrrry* sad. And then he went to this great workshop, and it was very much helping him.'

Tempering my scepticism, I at least want to give it a try. This is how I find myself in a small clammy room with six Indian women who like me are there to study Pranayama healing. All of us in search of answers. In the corner, our guru, Lakshmi, her mustard-coloured sari draped over her back, pours a cup of salt into a large plastic bowl filled with water.

'First you must try to feel your energy centre.' Lakshmi's velvety voice floats around us, a calming breeze on turbulent seas. 'Keep looking at the bowl. No thinking about nothing else.' She straightens up and closes her eyes. Pressing her palms together, she touches her third eye, the one on the middle of her forehead just between her eyebrows.

'This chakra is our sixth sense,' she says, 'and we need to unblock it.' She breathes in and lets out a *woosh* of air – a wave pounding the beach. 'This is the sense that helps us to see clearly, do away with negativity, and connect us to our gut feelings.' She opens her eyes and looks around the room. 'Just follow me. Do what I do.' She arches her back. 'Place your tongue against the roof of your mouth and focus here,' Lakshmi says, pointing at the bowl with salt water. She looks like a ballet dancer with outstretched arms.

The tip of my tongue strains against the roof of my mouth and I glue my eyes on the bowl as if I'm a magician trying to cast a spell. I try to concentrate and block out other thoughts, desperate to bring a positive change in my mood. But all I can see is John's face floating on the surface of the water. I try to dismiss the image, imagining him slipping into the air like the smoke on top of Aladdin's magic lantern, but he stares stubbornly back at me like a puppy waiting to be cuddled.

Lakshmi senses I'm struggling. She tiptoes towards me. 'Don't lose your focus now,' she whispers, waving her arms from the direction of the bowl towards my forehead. Her gold bangles tinkle. 'If you practice this daily, you will have good appetite, cheerfulness, handsome figure, good strength, courage, enthusiasm, a high standard of health, vigour and vitality and a very good concentration of mind.'

'Sweep your affliction from yourself into the bowl,' Lakshmi adds confidently, touching each of us one by one on the top of our heads. Her voice never falters. 'Feel your energy and cheerfulness return. But please, you must do this every day to get results.'

Her glowing complexion, soft smile and lustrous hair are a testament to her beliefs. She looks so healthy, calm and peaceful. 'Yogic breathing and salt water will change your life.' Her convictions are contagious, but salt water in a bowl feels like a sorcerer's fantasy. Am I wasting a day on a load of bullshit?

Four hours later, huddled over lunch, we women admit not feeling any different, even though Lakshmi announces that our auras are glowing more brightly.

'You are looking so much more radiant now.' Lakshmi hugs me when I leave. 'I know you are very much sceptical, but you will see. It does work.'

I know salt absorbs water moisture. That salt when rubbed into a tablecloth takes out red wine stains. But how can it possibly soak up the pain of John's death?

'Thank you. I will try,' I say as I leave.

The following morning, while the world is waking up, we 'yogi students' sit cross-legged on the lawn outside my block of flats here in Mumbai, overlooking the Indian Ocean. In the distance, crows caw, dogs bark and car alarms wail.

Draped in violet robes, the yoga guru blows on his conch and calls on the sun god to sanctify the yoga practice. The echoes hang in the muggy air. Then he calls on the gods to bless his students. I can't understand most of the Hindi chanting, but my neighbours are devotees. I try to hum along.

'Now you begin with the important chakra at the base of your spine,' the guru says. His booming voice makes the red petals on the hibiscus flowers flutter. 'You will begin to pump the anus. Today we focus on this chakra centre.'

Loud noises accompany this exercise, drowning out the sound of pounding waves breaking against the rocks. I giggle quietly instead of staying focused on my third eye, as the level of greenhouse gases around me increases. The sound of human wind crescendos, drowning the laughter of school kids walking by. At least I'm smiling again.

I wonder if all that hot air might also take on a different spiritual meaning, by injecting positive energy into my life. Sitting cross-legged on my yoga mat, all I feel are small stones and tufts of grass digging into my buttocks. Then I take in a deep belly breath, pinch my nostrils and join in the orchestra.

The class ends with the boat pose. While we lie on our backs, the guru urges us to imagine that we're floating on water. We raise our heads, arms and legs in the air and flop them against the ground, pumping our *mulibanda*, the area around the anus, again and again. Each time, our guru sings out claims to a better life.

'You are dropping your stress, you are dropping your anger, you are dropping your sorrows, you are dropping your personality defects.' His voice echoes across the gardens. 'The sea will wash them away.'

All the above characteristics infect me. Depression, despondency and denial. If only I can leave them behind. A black butterfly with white spots lands briefly on the back of my hand. Is it John calming me? Is he blowing the sweet fragrance from pink frangipani blossoms across me?

'You will now remain calm all day, not get stressed and not shout.' Those are the guru's parting prayers. His insistence sounds as if it comes with a life-time warranty.

Disorientated from all the breathing and chakra anal

pumping, the ground sways when I try to stand, so I sit down again. When I feel back in balance, I rise up and walk back to the entrance to my block of flats, not hearing the honking school buses and chattering schoolchildren. I get into the lift in my building and press the button for the wrong floor. As soon as I realise what I've done, I quickly I turn around and thrust my hand back between the doors to stop them from closing. The doors clamp down on my wrist as if they're guillotine knives about to slice it off. They don't have sensors to open again.

Now, I think to myself. *You're to be punished physically as well as emotionally. Have I been that bad a mother? What about the time I complained to John about his snoring?*

My arm is in a vice. I can almost see the blood spurting from my severed wrist. *How could I have been so stupid to stick out my arm?* I'm stuck. All I can do is pump my anus chakra. Closing my eyes, I take the deepest conscious breath I've taken since asbestos gutted John's lungs. Just then, Lakshmi's compassionate touch relaxes my shoulder. The salt water stares back at me as I focus all my energy on her imaginary bowl. Am I hallucinating? The bowl is now turquoise and not white. My rigid tongue softens and I taste the salt dripping down my perspiring face.

I can't find the air to yell for help. Instead, I wiggle my arm up and down. It seems to take minutes, although it's probably only a second or two to ease my hand out of the elevator's clutches. I rub my wrist, shake my hand, and exhale. It will bruise and swell, but all I care about is that my arm is in one piece.

Maybe the breathing relaxed the muscles in my forearm just enough for me to ease it out the door's rubber lining;

maybe the guru's prayers settled me into a positive mind-set; or maybe Lakshmi has indeed brought my aura to life? Just then I don't care what the reason is.

By evening, the swelling in my wrist is down. The bruises paler. For the first night in months there are no nightmares of John struggling to breathe as his lungs collapse. The cumulative effect of yoga and breathing exercises calms me.

The following morning, I wake to the sound of the conch vibrating across the lawn and look out at the sunrise, aglow in a vibrant hue of crimson. Holding the downward-facing dog position, my breathing feels longer, deeper and stronger. Even years later, after my daily yoga practice, there it is again. An image wafts around me. The bowl of saltwater, Laksmi's soothing voice and her tender touch.

Who would've thought that practical, down-to-earth me would get caught up in auras, meditative breathing and chanting? Or that the call of the conch would ease my tight neck muscles and seduce me into group healing yoga on the lawn, or prepare me for multi-religious immersions in Pushkar's holy temple and mosque? Or that I might even have a rare chance to meet with my grandfather's ghost?

CHAPTER 10

A Priest, an Imam and a Rabbi's Ghost

Draped in maroon robes, standing tall, with shoulder-length hair falling over his shoulders, the heavy-set priest bends down and gathers the cloth around his ankles with one hand. With the other, he dips a tin mug into Lake Pushkar's holy waters. His bare feet make a squelching sound on the slime-covered steps. He lifts the cup to the height of his eyes. Chanting what sounds like a blessing, he stares at me.

I gulp. *Will I really have to drink this murky water?* I swallow again, louder. The sound echoes in the space around me, and Anil, a colleague, turns to look at me.

I want to run. From this ceremony. From this holy man. From myself. From grief.

A ripple on the water's surface distracts me. Something tugs at a floating rose petal. A water-serpent, perhaps? Surely that's the only living thing that can survive in that scummy, algae-infested water. There it is again. A definite ripple. This time I recognise a fish's gaping mouth, attached to a grey fin and a scaly body.

'There are so many fish in this lake,' Anil leans over and whispers. He knows I'm freaking out.

'*Satyam Shivan Sundaram*,' chants the holy Brahmin.

Anil joins in the refrain and nudges me with his elbow. 'If you are wanting to be protected from leprosy and skin sickness, and be beautiful, charming and wise, you must be chanting too,' he murmurs.

His wife Mena turns to look at me and smiles an 'it's okay' reassurance.

Lips tingling, I sing along with our small group, trying to remember the words to the repetitive chant, but all I can think about are the stomach and scalp diseases I'll get when the water touches my lips and soaks my hair. Detecting a few more fish swirling around bits of puffed rice or polystyrene, I rub the sides of my neck and my shoulders relax – enough to begin breathing normally again. Now that I know fish live in this holy lake, I'm ready to receive the priest's blessings. I'll survive the dousing. Survive my loss. Isn't this blessing loftier than any mere stomach parasites and skin rashes?

It seems that for a while I've been concerned only about my wellbeing instead of reflecting on my beliefs and values. It's time to delve into compassion, empathy and caring, rather than bemoaning my fate. And anyway, what on earth am I doing with my life? I should be pondering the complexities of my very existence, rather than worrying about surviving this ceremony. I need to think about my future in a different way. How to be a role model for the junior women in my company. How to best coach my executive colleagues to achieve their career and business goals. How to be a supportive mum to kids in their thirties and have fun with my grandkids.

On the steps of the fourteenth-century Brahma temple at the edge of the lake, where a scarlet spire towers over us like a warrior protecting us from evil, I hear my grandfather, Rabbi Leib, turn over in his grave. He watches a priest bless a widowed granddaughter, in a non-Jewish house of prayer, where people pray to idols. Although he died when I was three, at auspicious times like these, for some strange reason, I often think of him. Maybe because he was a man of God, had faith and believed in the Almighty.

If he could see me sitting in the shadows of Ganesh, the elephant God – and Hanuman, the monkey God...? I close my eyes and shiver in the heat. When I take my next breath I feel a heavenly breeze as if an angel has fallen from the skies to find Grandpa Leib, wearing a long black coat and yarmulke, standing next to me. 'Listen,' I whisper to myself as much as to him, 'as long as I can see these plump fish swallowing the rose petals we're throwing onto the water, I'm happy. I'm not going to be cursed or die from a few holy sprinkles.' He strokes his greying beard. 'I know,' I say. 'I should be thinking about our Jewish God, but right now I can't quite connect.' I pause before continuing. 'Maybe you're smart enough to know why it isn't enough for me to visit these holy places without receiving the priest's blessings?'

Grandpa mumbles a familiar Sabbath prayer. 'Blessed art thou, Lord our God, who brings forth bread from the earth.' I mouth the words after him in the same familiar sing-song chant. He looks down at me and continues saying *Kiddush* – the Jewish prayer over Sabbath wine. I move closer to him, but Grandpa turns his back and walks away. Even his shadow vanishes.

Sunlight reflects off white buildings lining the lake. Small waves lap at my feet. The priest motions me to sit on the step, lifts the mug over my head and tilts the rim to my lips. I lock my jaw. Water trickles down my face and back. I wipe my mouth, hoping no bacteria manage to breach my pursed lips and storm the palace entrance.

The familiar clop-clopping of the ever-present holy cow on the stone floor echoes across the marble edifice. I wait for it. The swishing steam, rancid odour and the trickle of urine. Plop. I spring up and slip on the green slime, almost losing my balance. If the sacred Pushkar Lake is going to heal and purify me, I don't want to sit near a puddle of poop.

In direct contrast to the pandemonium of the street market on the other side of the temple, the courtyard is quiet. Flies swarm and buzz around the cowpat. There is a swishing noise from the cow's tail, and a popping sound from the fishes' mouths as they break the surface of the water. Pink-toned palaces and apartment blocks gently caress the lake's circumference. Fifty-two bathing bays and steps, known as *ghats* are interspersed between the buildings. The gentle echo of a conch caresses devotees immersing themselves into the holy waters. In one bay women are swathed in saris, while in another, the men wear only loincloths.

'These pilgrims,' Anil points at the bathers, 'they travel so far to come here. Hundreds of miles by train and bus. Like us, they are making many wishes and hoping for many blessings.'

Mena's sodden violet-and-red-striped sari clings to her buxom hips. She covers her face with her hands, looks up at the heavens and whispers a repetitive chant. The rows of rainbow-coloured bangles on her forearms jangle as she prays.

I wonder what prayers she holds in her heart. I can't remember ever being blessed by a rabbi. We only pray to our invisible God. A spiritual heretic, I'm standing in the gently lapping waves, surrounded by true believers, sucked into the magic around me – the chanting, the drenching, the gifting to the gods, and the yearning for wishes to be granted.

I wish I knew what to wish for. All I want is for John to come back to me but that's an unrealistic fantasy. *Will this feeling of emptiness ever pass?*

A crow flaps its wings and caws its raucous approval as the priest dips his thumb into a small pot of coloured powder, presses a dark red *bindi* into my forehead, and ties a red cotton bangle around my wrist, the sign that I've *'done poojah'* – created a relationship with the divine. Sandalwood incense mingles with dung. I touch my *bindi* with my forefinger and lift the *poojah* bracelet to my mouth. I've no wish to connect to any god, but I begin to believe in belief itself. My own belief *in* myself.

Mena looks at me, smiles and takes my arm. 'You are a proper Indian now,' she says, touching her head against mine. 'Now we go to the very famous Adhai Din Ka Jhonpra Mosque just around the corner. I studied the structure of this mosque in my architect degree. It's very ancient, from over 1000 years BCE. Let's put on our sandals and walk over.'

Once we reach the entrance to this majestic house of prayer, Anil and I each receive a shocking-pink kerchief to cover our heads. Mena covers hers with her slate-blue pashmina and continues talking. 'There were once more than three hundred engraved pillars here, but now many are gone. It was built without cement, and still many domes remain.' She points up and around the ceiling arches. 'Even though we are Hindus, we love to come here, to the inner court. Look at all these stalls selling baskets of flowers – marigolds, purple irises, white carnations. We must each buy one basket.'

My senses are on fire. The religious fervour ignites the kaleidoscope of colour, the crowds of people. Inoffensive pushing, bumping, sweat and perfumes. *Have I been colour-blind my whole life?*

The mix of Indo-Islamic architecture greets us at every turn. On tapered floral and foliate patterns, inscriptions are engraved alongside quotations from the Koran. The innermost courtyard is similar to a Hindu temple, but I see no resemblance to the Dome of the Rock in Jerusalem or the Blue Mosque in Istanbul.

Mena continues authoritatively. 'This very unusual mosque was built by mostly Hindu masons for their Muslim masters.' She speaks softly, an eastern-educated architect to an eager-occidental student.

'That is why it is so very beautiful. Everything blends together with such ease.'

We're greeted by the imam, who asks us to throw our flowers into the centre of the inner court. I copy my friends and bow. When he lays his hands on my head, an inner calm fills me yet again. This time from another god.

'Are you Catholic or Methodist?' Anil whispers. He looks away when I tell him I'm Jewish. '*Ahh*, we thought you are Catholic.' Another conversation stopper.

Now I'm curious as to why my hosts come to be blessed in a mosque if they're Hindus, but feel it's impolite to ask.

As if he knows once more what's going through my mind, Anil leans towards me and puts his hand on my shoulder. 'We pray to everyone's gods. Sometimes we go to church, sometimes to temple, and every now and again to the mosque.' He waves his arms above his head as if fanning an angel's wings.

Anil's vermillion bindi grows darker. 'You know you are the first Jewish we have met,' he says, turning to Mena. 'Right, *Babu?*'

Now it's my turn to frown. I don't know what to say.

'Well, I'm happy to be the first at something,' I say, smiling. I feel myself blush and wish I could take the words back and say something more meaningful. 'When you come to Bombay I'll take you to the Jewish synagogue. It has a beautiful blue dome.'

'We'd love to.'

In this fusion of religious traditions and rituals, I become aware that my emotional discrepancies force me to hold one foot on the gas and the other on the brakes. I'm filled with a quest to live a full life as a widow – to find my own family, my own community and my own space. At times, John leans down from wherever he is and tugs me forward, encouraging me. At other times, bereft without him, I find no place in the world.

On our way out of the mosque, we pass through the 'Hall of the Homeless', where people lie around on filthy sheets. Matted, grimy, skinny. Despair oozes out of every pore amid shadowed, dull eyes. I know those eyes. Hollow like mine. It's time for a change. These destitute souls are shunned, outcast, hopeless. But I have a way out, a path for a different future.

Mena leads the way out of the shrouded hall, down a narrow passage, but the moans of the destitute follow me and dampen my courage. She turns around, grabs my elbow and ushers me forward.

'You're okay,' she says, blowing away the clouds of pain.

'We'll be out of all this in a minute.' Her voice, soft but strong, calms me as we shuffle along in slow motion.

A floodlight blinds me. We're at the exit, and I raise my hand to shade my eyes from the incandescent sunlight. Sunglasses don't dampen the glare.

Outside, the market lane heaves with shoppers and pilgrims jostling to buy trinkets, mementos and hijabs. Brass pots, aluminium pans, and blue and pink plastic buckets line the narrow pavement. On large steel wall hooks burgundy floral Muslim prayer mats cluster amongst caps, scarves and T-shirts from Manchester United, Arsenal and Chelsea football clubs. Statues of Ganesh – the god of new beginning and remover of obstacles – fill the shelves.

I buy a copper moulding of the elephant god that fits in the palm of my hand and wrap it in a red and white Arsenal scarf and a magenta hijab. As I stuff my purchases into my tote, two Hassidic men wearing long black coats and broad black felt hats brush past me and turn off the next corner.

What on earth are they doing here? Then I see a sign on the wall. Chabad House.

'See,' I say to Anil and Mena. 'Those two men are Jewish from a very religious sect.' I point at the sign of the star of David on a nearby wall. 'That is a Jewish learning and study centre.'

But I don't tell them that Grandpa Leib is here with me, wagging his disapproving index finger. Strange. No wonder I fit in so well. Like this cultural mélange, I'm riddled with so many contradictions, I could fill the *Book of Susan*.

CHAPTER 11

Genesis on the Ganges

Dodging branches of bananas and piles of steaming cowpats, I join swarms of Hindu pilgrims surging towards a platform known as a *ghat* on the banks of the river Ganges.

On this sultry evening in Varanasi, the spiritual capital of India, where wisps of burnt orange float along the horizon, and gods greet departed souls, I merge with the throngs rushing towards the ritual evening prayers. As smoke from funeral pyres sweeps into a fading steel-blue sky, I'm compelled to plunge into the crowds. In this city devoted to dying and death, I'm here to say my goodbye.

Cows amble unflustered amongst us in the ancient labyrinth. From time to time, these sacred animals pause to nudge through baskets piled high with spinach, potatoes or garlic bulbs in search of a snack. No one seems to mind the disarray created by these revered providers of milk and ghee.

All around me, long, wavy hair bobs on fuchsia, sapphire and silver scarves. Bangles jingle. Sandals clatter. Hips sway, revealing glimpses of soft flesh. Men lift their long tunics so they can run faster. Trousers swish. Engulfed in the pungent aroma of marigolds, I sprint along with them. My cerise silk pantaloons billow in the breeze and my flip-flops slosh in between the damp cobbled stones.

My American travel companions who flew over to visit me opted to stay behind at our serene luxury hotel. They can't understand why I'm prepared to jostle with bicycle rickshaws and fight off aggressive market vendors when I can enjoy the sunset in peace and quiet, sipping wine on the balcony overlooking the Ganges.

'Bring back some good pictures,' Peter says, uncorking a bottle of Chardonnay. Jane, his wife, brushes her blonde hair over her shoulders and lifts her feet onto a leather footstool. Her crimson nail polish glints in the fading light. She laughs at me as I stuff my camera into my backpack next to my orange pashmina.

'Watch out for cow pats and steer clear of all those bikes and rickshaws. Let us know when you're back safe and sound.' She raises her glass. *'L'chaim –* to life.'

Surrounded by palaces, priests, and prayers, I'm not tempted to change my plans. At first, I'd been overwhelmed, like Jane – scared and even intimidated by the circuitry of overloaded sensory stimulation in the city's sacred hullabaloo. I held up my arms to screen myself from persistent hawkers and pinched my nose at the invasive smell of ammonia from the public toilets. A holy man with a white striped face, fierce eyes and a long unruly beard grabbed my arm and pulled me towards him. I stepped back and yelped.

'No, no,' I said, 'leave me,' and wiped my contaminated arm with my scarf as if that would save me from the plague.

But when I learned that Buddha delivered his first sermon here, I saw faith in a different light. The divine presence of the compassionate and loyal monkey god, Hanuman, floated over me as I stood on the steps of his vermillion Nepali Temple. My body tingled from my neck to my thighs. I didn't move until Jane whispered, 'Hey, there is a line behind you.'

The shrines in every courtyard and nook of this town begin to comfort me, a Jewish widow, in an invisible embrace. Now, I want to submerge myself in the ceremony of lights and attempt to discover the nirvana that's evaded me since John's death. I want to breathe in all the life around me, stop feeling utterly alone, and stop fearing my loneliness.

In this city of death, I have my chance to come back to life.

Living in India has revived my senses and brought me back into an animated and flamboyant world. I see scarlet, maroon and crimson instead of merely red chillies. I can smell and taste the difference between an Alphonso, the queen of mangoes – sugary, pulpy and fragrant – and the firm Bombay Green, used only in chutney. The distinct flavours of food have begun to stand out to me – rosemary, curry leaves, cumin and pepper, rather than simply curry.

I relish the new life I've begun to build away from home. How odd things have turned out. So different from the traditional world that John and I dreamed about and planned together – evenings at the theatre, walks on Hampstead Heath, and Sunday brunches of poached eggs and bacon with the kids. I wonder how I'll ever be able to move back home to London and join the grey-suited corporate ranks again.

After a year living and working in India, I've changed, moulting my shyness. Straining out of my grief-stricken chrysalis, I've fluttered back into the universe – making new friends riding on overcrowded trains, sharing samosas and masala omelettes, and even enjoying the fierce bargaining with hawkers in the local market. Laughing and shaking hands as we agree on a price, which I know is much higher than the locals pay.

In a clearing near the Ganges, a funeral pyre spews psychedelic orange and red ambers into the sooty sky. Flames singe hair, then skin and flesh. Bodies hiss. The thin veil between life and death floats in the smoke. Relatives, heads bowed, sway and chant as they call out their goodbyes and offer final prayers. Irrationally, I wish I'd brought John here towards his end to join these souls in transit to paradise.

Our children and I had been with him in our bedroom when he took his last breath. But John had been so alone when his chest lay naked under the coroner's knife in a mortuary reeking of bleach when death made a stranger of his face. And when his mutilated body slid down the chute into the sealed crematorium's oven, there'd been no time for another, final goodbye. Here, surrounded by holy sanctuaries, where the gods release a person's soul and provide an assurance of heavenly bliss, it isn't too late for John to rest in peace.

When I reach the *ghat*, the sky has lost the sunset hues and I manage to squeeze into the only small space on a stone bench. Sticky limbs press against me. My kurta sticks to my back. Thighs touch. Ignoring the organised turmoil on its banks, the most worshipped and one of the most polluted rivers on earth, continues unperturbed on its thousand-mile journey to the Bay of Bengal. There it spreads its many arms, stretching into a two-hundred-mile delta en route to the ocean. Corpses, sewage and chemical waste bob along, unnoticed and unheeded on the khaki-coloured current.

On the holy waters tourists in canoe-like boats decorated with candles and marigolds drift by like fallen leaves. Men in loincloths soap their bodies until they're covered in white foam. Then, as if to wash away their sins, they hold their noses and dunk themselves in the river.

Not far away, women draped in magenta and ochre saris dip themselves in the holy water alongside floating wooden planks, laden with cremated remains and dead bodies wrapped in pumpkin-coloured fabric. A woman struggles to disentangle a plastic bag from her dripping hair. I knew The Ganges was polluted, but I didn't expect to see so much rubbish; pieces of cloth, condoms and tampons weaving amidst the submerged worshipers. The smell of caustic effluents from the leather tanneries and sulphuric acid catches the back of my throat. Safe on my seat, I'm not brave enough to quickly dip a finger or toe in the holy water.

Framed by the blazing, sinking sun, two tall, imposing priests in turmeric-hued robes step onto a small platform. Wide belts shape their waists, leaving their muscular chests partially exposed. The soft echo of a conch, followed by a sacred silence, subdues the oppressive cacophony. The bombardment of honking horns, screeching tyres and shouting vendors lessens and then ceases. The evening prayer rites begin.

Each priest lifts two lanterns and begins to chant. The rhythms have a distinct beat, modified by pauses and emphasis on certain words. I hum to the calming, repetitive refrains. The priests wave their hands in large circles as if they are gods directing me to paradise. Their robes slip open just a tad more. I haven't a clue what they're reciting, but I finally manage to join haltingly in the refrain.

On a purely gut level, I feel these holy men are holding my destiny in their outstretched arms. It's as if they're telling me that I will laugh, and maybe even love and be loved again. Nourished by scents, chants, colours and fragrances, my spirit can be reborn.

The chanting rises to a crescendo, reminiscent of a cantor leading the liturgical singing in a synagogue. For the first time in years, a tune bubbles up my throat. My sense of isolation lessens as my neighbours on either side take my hands and raise my wrists into the air.

Bells ring out, and the rhythmic beating of a nearby drum joins the vibrant chorus. My eyes moisten. Was this the way the Jews had felt when Moses came down from Mount Sinai carrying the tablets? But what about the downside?

Sucked into the fervour, I grit my teeth, seeing images of Hitler hypnotising his audiences near the Brandenburg Gate. I feel uneasy and part of me looks for the exit sign. But I stick with it. This is why I'm here.

I close my eyes in an attempt to immerse myself in the intoxicating drama and seek my own Jewish God. My latent spirituality blossoms as I enter into an unfamiliar intimacy with an alien world. I breathe in the fragrance of marigolds – half alluring, half unpleasantly pungent. Sandalwood incense wafts into the dark sky and lifts me onto a smoky cloud.

On this auspicious evening, I take in the crackle of the firewood and the stench of burning bodies as part of tradition, strangely freed from the angst I felt when John's coffin slid down a ramp into the crematorium. Twisting my wedding ring, now on the third finger of my left hand, I hear John telling me it's okay to try to wave goodbye.

The heavenly backdrop behind the priests turns grey, then black. Entranced by the raw sensuality of the religious theatre all around me, my cheeks burn. I realise that I haven't once thought to take my camera out of my backpack. I've become a participant in a religious ceremony rather than a foreigner taking photos. John's death and my life are part of the melding horizon of endings and beginnings. The veil between life and death is as thin and fragile as a butterfly's wing. At those crossroads, where life and death embrace each other with so much openness, I'm cradled by a world of believers.

I came to India alone and afraid, and now I am part of the Great Tableau. Part of history. Part of life.

CHAPTER 12

Shedding Widow's Weeds

'We have no help here if we're getting a puncture,' Khamat says. 'The road is very bad.'

We're driving on the Port Road to the Afghan church for a Remembrance Day service, to commemorate the contribution of British and Commonwealth servicemen during the two world wars.

Fountains of dust invade our air-conditioned car. In my comfortable five-star bubble, I ignore Khamat's warning. The thought of taking an extra hour on the only main gridlocked, tarred artery is unappealing. Besides, I'm seeing another side of Mumbai life. The 'backside'. The Port Road.

'Don't worry,' I assure him with no basis. 'We'll be fine. I'm sure we'll find someone to help us if we need to.'

Role reversal.

Khamat doesn't understand why I've begun to enjoy living beyond my comfort zone – hiking with the team in their twenties and thirties in the nearby mountains up to Peb Fort where I scale ladders installed against the vertical rock-face. At dawn I stroll along the banks of the Panje-Dongri wetlands in Navi Mumbai scanning for sand plovers, flamingos, ruddy

115

shelducks, bee-eaters, purple moorhens and pipers. Khamat is upset to learn that I climbed onto the roof of the learning centre with the contractor to search for the crack in the leaking roof.

'It's not safe for you,' he says, like a disapproving parent, clucking his tongue on the roof of his mouth. 'You must not be doing all these things.'

Pulling my hair back into a hair clip, I nod but ignore his advice. Now I wish I hadn't.

The steering wheel jerks Khamat's hands to the left and right as we lurch in and out of unavoidable potholes. Gravel crackles under the tyres. I sink into the back seat, preparing to submit my spine to reckless punishment.

Unable to steady my hands, the *Times of India* newspaper wobbles from side to side. Instead of trying to catch up on the war in Iraq, I allow my imagination to float back a hundred, maybe two hundred years when Britannia ruled the waves and Mumbai's port had been a cornerstone of Queen Victoria's great empire. In the 1800s, huge warehouses brimmed with bales of fluffy cotton. Coffee beans, and rolls of coloured silks and satins spilled out of hemp sacks. Sheds lining the coast, hemmed in by marshes on the one side and the Indian Ocean on the other, housed crates of pepper, salt, fenugreek, cloves and a variety of teas that filled the holds of cargo ships sailing to their British conquerors. Bombay, as it was known then, had been a bustling, efficient, imperialist moneymaking machine. All the while, the Brits drained the country's resources and taxed the locals into desperation.

Now, black smudges from centuries of monsoon mould and pollution smother these once-bustling sheds. Rats scamper over piles of neglected sacks whose gaping mouths spew out mouldy black beans, walnut-brown lentils and grey rice. A man urinates onto the wheel over a stationary truck. A child squats, defecating amongst the tawny oxen, wagons and rubble.

As if it were a mirage in the Great Indian Desert, a large sandy field suddenly appears in the midst of the squalor. A freshly painted signpost points to THE CRICKET CLUB, where groups of boys and men wielding wooden sticks for bats and rags for balls are bowling and batting. It's possible to play cricket anywhere with anything. *Thwack!* Bails fall off the wicket stumps, and someone yells, '*Yay*. He's out!'

Huge open concrete drains filled with grimy-green sludge edge towards the sea. Like Kipling's Elephant's Child standing on the banks of the great grey-green, greasy Limpopo River, I'm filled with the same 'insatiable curiosity'. Later I come to understand that this long drive buried in history will become a turning point for me to understand that like those cricket players, I, as a widow, can and will find a space to play.

Unscrewing the top off my water bottle, I gulp, swish the liquid around my mouth and swallow. The film of dust on my tongue disappears. The road narrows to one lane. Branches of banyan trees with wrinkled roots high above the ground scrape the sides of the car as we ease our way past a large military compound surrounded by imposing walls topped with concertina barbed wire.

Around the next corner, the Afghan church – a commanding Victorian cathedral – straddles the middle of the road. This bastion of imperialism with its sixty-five-foot bell tower challenges us to halt to the sound of bugles, flutes and drums. An Indian army orchestra stands on a bandstand playing popular World War I songs – 'Keep the Home Fires Burning' and 'It's a Long Way to Tipperary'. Sweat pours down the faces of the stoic musicians wearing heavy serge khaki uniforms. Bagpipes squawk at the beginning of 'Abide with Me'.

In the church courtyard, women from the British Embassy, pale cheeks flushed under caked makeup and smelling of talcum powder, join balding white men wearing white shirts, dark suits and black ties. They dot the lawn, like so many wild dandelions, and clap softly at the end of each song. In another group, Indian women swagger in maroon, cobalt and mauve saris, while the members of the Indian military wear neatly pressed khakis with high boots covering long socks. Rows of military medals straddle aging military chests.

Chatter stops. Drums roll and trumpets blare to 'Onward Christian Soldiers, marching as to war...' A flock of green parrots flies off from the gargoyles, screeching, as if they're complaining about the hymn selection. I don't blame them. It seems somewhat inappropriate given that many Hindus, Jains, Sikhs and Muslims also lost their lives at Dunkirk, at the Khyber Pass and Gallipoli.

A line of buglers and trombonists, pied pipers in crisp cream uniforms, play 'The Last Post', as they lead us in a procession to the church nave. Tall gothic arches framed by towering stained-glass windows rise to the heavens. Soft-pink and dull-blue hues of basalt, marble and limestone glow, as streaks of golden sunlight float through the tinctured panes of coloured glass.

This imposing Gothic structure is a smaller but no less impressive version of Gloucester Cathedral. A plaque on the wall explains that this edifice was built by India's British rulers in 1847, to commemorate the slaughter of a British battalion in the Hindu Kush and Kandahar, by Afghan forces. No images connect the church's name to Afghanistan. Not the architecture, the remembrance plaques, the stained-glass windows nor the pews. No Perso-Arabic script decorates the arches.

The Indian national anthem echoes from the buglers' mouths like a low murmur, a croon, a cry, as if reading the letters filled with the evocative language of cultural dislocation and tragedy, sent by Indian soldiers in France and Belgium to their families in villages back home.

The muscles in my neck tense. I hope they won't play 'God Save the Queen'.

Speeches begin. For the first time, I learn of the two and a half million Indian infantry who served in both world wars in far-off lands alongside their British oppressors.

Brigadier Furdoon S. B. Metha gives a speech, emphasising how little has been written about his comrades' sacrifices. He describes how during the First World War Indian soldiers went to Europe in their tropical cotton drill. Winter kit, including greatcoats, didn't arrive in time to save dozens perishing from cold and frostbite. Racial attitudes of that era treated Indian fighters as inferiors. Hospitalised Indian soldiers in places such as Brighton weren't provided direct care from English nurses, and recuperating troops were kept under armed guard in locked camps. Those turbaned soldiers who fought in the same trenches as the *Tommies* were forgotten. Back in India, they were then ostracised by their communities and seen as having served an unworthy cause.

While the suffering of the Indian infantry was undeniable, all I can think of is their widows who, left with nothing, were shunned and isolated. Although my situation is much easier, I can still identify with some aspects of what those widows went through. Here, in India, mentioning that my husband died is often a conversation stopper. In London, after John died, many of our friends dropped me, preferring that I meet with 'wives only'. Most of my friends now are either single women or widows.

This memorial service helps me realise that it's up to me to try to overcome this stigma. After all, I have a profession, a career and am free to choose where and how I'd like to live my life. If I could only grasp this freedom and let go of my dour self-perception, this transition could be a new beginning. My choice is to stay stuck or take a brave step and make my own new world. This revelation thrills and scares me. In my pew with my wavy shoulder-length hair, wrists laden with rose-red and orange bangles, and long drop imitation-jade earrings, I'm convinced that there's no going back to my earlier London life, as it was – navy and black suits with cream blouses. But I feel stuck. I can't move forward, either.

The service ends with Psalm number 23, 'The Lord is my Shepherd'. Then the congregation strolls back into the garden to enjoy Earl Grey tea in bone-china cups and saucers under fragrant pink blossoms of frangipani trees. We make small talk and snack on ham-and-cheese rolls and chicken sandwiches on sliced white bread with no crusts. No chai, no samosas and no kulfi ice cream in sight.

As if we've taken a step back in time, to the days of the Raj, the Europeans and the Indians stand distant in separate small groups. My fuchsia kurta puts me firmly in the local camp. But with my white skin, where will I be accepted and where do I belong?

Like the Afghan church, I no longer fit into one category. Not uniquely South African – my birthplace. Nor Israeli – where I lived for twenty years as a young mother. Nor British. But a mix of all three. As for religion: Jewish, but not religious, and open to the offerings of all faiths. How can I come to terms with these inconsistencies when most other people I know belong to only one country, religion or race? I take my chances and decide to spend time in both camps. I enjoy spending time with people who are different than I.

It no longer matters that I don't fit in a box. I'm learning to cross human borders and gain the freedom to navigate between generations, religions and customs, even if there are times when I feel ill at ease.

The Brits talk about their plans for Christmas, Sunday lunches of roast beef and Yorkshire pudding at the club, and how Gordon Brown encourages foreign investment into the UK. I nibble on finger sandwiches that taste like cotton wool. Then I find the courage to join a much younger group from the Indian military. Their discussion focuses on the recent violence in Kashmir. To them, it doesn't matter that I'm single, a widow or from London.

'You must come for dinner this evening,' insists Seema, a colonel's wife.

'I'd love to,' I say as she leans forward to kiss me on the cheek.

Here in this gathering of cultures and histories, I begin to make some sense of the next phase of my life, finding my unique place in the world. It's all in reach.

No longer an interloper, I could be a *Mumbaikar* (a resident of Mumbai) munching *vada pav* from street vendors. I could wear gold and silver necklaces and two-inch-drop earrings. I could take belly-dancing and salsa classes and enjoy Bollywood movies in reclining cinema seats. Expansive, untangled and unconstrained.

Suddenly, the thought strikes me like a ball off a cricket bat. I can find joy again. Even without John.

CHAPTER 13

The Mumbai Massacre

Day 1: My Mumbai flat

The 26th of November, 2008 begins as a typical Mumbai evening. Mothers kiss their children goodnight, set their alarm clocks and bid their servants a pleasant evening. Flats turn dark. At Chabad House, a Jewish learning centre, and home to the Holtzberg family, two-year-old Moshe dozes off, sucking on his pacifier. A nightlight glows near his crib so that he won't be scared of the dark.

No one has a clue that the benign hubbub of India's cosmopolitan city is about to be shattered. Not the security men leaning against poles, chatting at hotel entrances. Not the families licking soft smooth ice cream on Marine Drive. Not the young lovers perched on large boulders gazing at the rising moon. No one notices a dinghy bearing ten men from Pakistan, members of the Islamic terror group Lashkar-e-Tayyiba, as it sneaks through a maze of fishermen's boats.

Armed with hand grenades, AK-47s, Colts, machine guns and satellite phones, the gunmen clamber onto shore. They fan out through the downtown tourist and commercial districts, targeting popular hotels and restaurants, shooting at anyone in their way.

Explosions rip through the city and a smell of burning fills the air. From my Mumbai flat, I watch an orange cloud rise above the smog. My hand shakes as I pick up the remote to turn on the TV. A cameraman shows a scene of the invaders firing randomly at thousands of people at Chhatrapati Shivaji, the city's major train station.

Fumbling with the cap on a bottle of water, I drain it in a single gulp. The terrorists struck right at the heart of the modern acropolis. I crush the water bottle in my hand and throw it into the bin.

Numerous armed conflicts between India and Pakistan have erupted since the end of British rule in 1947 – skirmishes and military standoffs – fighting over Kashmir's sovereignty near the northern border. But this is different. Near my office *and* my home.

A terrorist spokesman calls into the newsroom and shouts above the din. 'We want you must release all the Pakistani mujahedeen, our Islamic brothers that your government is holding in jail in India. Until we have them we looking for Britishers, the Israeelees and Americans. This is no joking.' Before his location can be traced, he cuts off the call from his satellite phone.

Hand grenades explode in the lobbies and corridors of five-star hotels. Smoke triggers fire alarms. People scream and dive for cover, trying to dodge the bullets. They scurry under tables, hide behind curtains, and duck behind the chicken and goat carcasses in kitchen freezers. Texts and tweets beg for help. Guests hide in wardrobes, cowering behind shower curtains and beneath beds.

The local police and army struggle to coordinate a response. Newscasters bellow above the explosions.

'You can see the Taj Mahal Hotel, it is burning,' a distraught reporter cries as she slithers across the compound on her belly, a soldier under fire, her face barely visible through the smoke. 'My God,' she sputters, 'there are so many people in that inferno. In there dying. Someone just jumped out a window.'

The legendary hotel lobby with its plush Persian carpets and ionic columns is a war zone. I'd been there only a few hours earlier with Vijay, my company's director of operations. Over a feast of potato samosas, lentil soup, curried vegetables, chilli crab, saffron rice and fresh coconut we'd outlined plans for a leadership workshop.

The city is in lockdown, those plans are gone.

I know what it's like to be under attack. Trapped, unprepared and terrified. I lived as a young wife and mother near Tel Aviv during the outbreak of the 1973 Yom Kippur war, when Egyptian tanks crossed the Suez Canal determined to destroy the Jewish state. Those wailing ambulance sirens in Mumbai – rushing the wounded and dying to emergency hospital rooms – sound all too familiar.

When invaders from Lebanon hijacked a bus towards the city and then escaped into nearby orange groves, my son and daughter, both under the age of four, were asleep in their bedroom. I'd sat alone in the dark living room of our small house, a revolver in my lap, cringing at the slightest noise.

Now, in my Mumbai living room, watching the horror on television, this attack feels different. Maybe because I feel so isolated and alone in a foreign country. This time, will I survive?

I close my eyes, unnerved that I might not see my kids and grandchildren again. Fixated by the nearby flames, I step out onto my veranda and lean over the rusty railings. I'm the only white person in my sprawling block of flats, and the terrorists will find me easily by threatening the receptionist at the gate. I'm an obvious target. What will I do or where will I go if I need help? I wipe my clammy palms on my T-shirt.

Day 2: The Israeli consul's flat

Early that morning, I learn that the terrorists invaded Chabad house, home to Rabbi Gabi, his wife Rivka and baby Moshe. Images of them raping Rivka and torturing Gabi wash through my mind. How could two-year-old Moshe survive?

I call my friend Hannah, who works at the consulate.

'Why aren't our security guys going in?'

It takes a while for her to respond. When she does, her voice is hoarse. 'The Indian army and police won't let us near the place. We don't want a political incident on top of everything else.'

I push my palm into my forehead. 'Sorry, that was a stupid question.'

'Look,' Hannah says, 'Can you get over here and give us a hand? I've been on the phone for hours. I could really use a break.'

Me? When the city is in lockdown? It's dangerous out there with terrorists around every corner.

A loud bang erupts through the phone and I instinctively duck, covering my head with my hands.

'Are you okay?'

'*Y-y-yes*. I think.' She pauses. 'Can you hurry?'

'I'm on my way.' I say the words as much to bolster my own morale as hers.

Dangerous or not. She needs me. And I'll just go crazy cooped up here on my own anyway. Waiting. Hoping.

When I call Khamat and ask him to take me to the Israel consul's flat, he hesitates.

'Okay,' he says after a long pause, 'I will take you. And then come back to my family. You can phone me again tonight, and I'll come and bring you home.'

* * *

The sounds we experience on the drive to meet Hannah are different than normal. No school buses chugging by. No sound of children laughing and chatting. No planes screaming across the sky. Even the crows are silent. The only sounds are television and radio broadcasts blaring out of buildings and car windows in languages I don't understand. The roads are nearly empty. No fighting heavy commuter traffic today. Khamat listens to the radio and translates some of the news. I put my elbow against the window and recall my recent evening with the Holtzbergs. Singing, clapping, laughing.

The couple welcomes anyone who wants to practice Judaism to Chabad House. Or to take the mikvah – a ritual bath – eat kosher food, or simply meet other Jews and Israelis. The Holtzbergs don't distinguish between secular and ultra-religious folk. An atheist Jewish woman, I've long given up on religion and don't wish to feel any pressure to attend synagogue

127

services. But, I do follow tradition and enjoy celebrating Jewish holidays with the local Mumbai community.

Although my grandfather had been a rabbi in Volksrust – a small town in South Africa – my parents focused on the importance of strong family values rather than the Orthodox traditions of what to eat and wear. It's been decades since I attended synagogue, and then only for my son's bar mitzvah. I never did see the point in praying in ancient Hebrew – a language I don't understand. I've even developed a prejudice against ultra and Orthodox Jewish elements – annoyed by their views and behaviour towards women as second-class citizens.

It was a leap for me to join the Holtzbergs for Friday-night Sabbath dinners. Once a guest in their home, I realised that they were far more tolerant of others' religious beliefs and opinions than I am, disappointed in myself for holding such a biased worldview. The couple is charming, hospitable and friendly, even to infidels like me. I feel guilty that it took a while for me to accept them for who they are, as good people, rather than stereotype them as religious fundamentalists.

Recently, I joined the Holtzbergs in the courtyard at Chabad House to celebrate Sukkoth with some Jewish and Israeli friends, commemorating the forty years the Jews spent in the desert after escaping slavery in Egypt. We feasted on typical Israeli dishes – hummus, tahini, falafel, pitta and barbecued chicken in the Chabad Centre's courtyard. We devoured meze seasoned with fennel, oregano, garlic and coriander. Linking arms, we sang Israeli songs as we swayed left to right. Baby Moshe clapped his hands and toddled around in circles until his nappy fell to his knees. His giggles rose above the singing until he stumbled, half asleep, into his young mother's lap.

I felt good bonding so closely with the Jewish and Israeli community – the Jewish jokes, the Hebrew slang, the common love of Jerusalem's old city and the piquant cuisine.

The day following the attack, I join Hannah and a group of Israelis in the consul's living room. Legs cross, uncross and cross again. I bite a piece of loose skin on my cuticle, go to the bathroom and try not to keep twirling my hair. The consul checks her Blackberry like a nurse monitoring an ECG. No one talks. Eyes fixed on the television, we wait for more news about the Holtzbergs. Intermittent blasts resound across the city as the terrorists continue their carnage. Hundreds of hostages are stuck in the smoking hotels – including a number of delegates from the European Parliament.

Amit, a member of the Israeli team, rushes into the consul's living room. He appears flushed.

'Apparently the terrorists know that there is a high-profile EU meeting here in Mumbai. These guys planned their timing.' He stares at a computer printout in his hand. His voice cracks. 'I… I have a report.' He pauses, reading. 'In addition to the Holtzbergs, many well-known politicians are in danger. No one seems to know if they're okay.'

He drops his hands. Amit lets out a deep sigh. Dark stains appear under the armpits of his blue denim shirt.

Addicted to the news, we sit erect on leather couches. Television cameras spare no grisly details. They focus on people fleeing the main train terminus. Porters, accustomed to hoisting heavy loads on their heads, lie slumped on the ground. Satchels, fingers, flip-flops, feet, magazines, mobiles, glasses, newspapers, ears, laptops, legs and Cadbury's chocolate bars desecrate the platforms.

Scenes from Leopold's restaurant, where I often enjoy tandoori chicken and vegetable biryani, unfold before me. Diners shot while mopping naan bread into masala gravy defy description. Splintered beer bottles and curry sauces spilled onto the floor streaked with blood paint the television screen with death. I run to the bathroom trying not to retch.

'You can't believe how well equipped these people are,' the English news broadcaster sputters. He removes his tie, wipes his brow and opens the top button of his crumpled shirt. 'They have hand grenades and automatic weapons. They're attacking the luxury hotels – the Taj Mahal and Oberoi, and also Leopold's. They're looking especially for foreigners and tourists.' He swallows. 'We don't know yet what's happening at the Jewish house. The police are there, but they haven't yet issued any statements. The situation here seems to be dire.'

Outside our window, smoke hovers in the azure sky. Again, I pick at the cuticle of my thumb until it bleeds before I wrap it in a tissue. Is it really possible that no one has any idea of what's happening? When it will all end? Even the army spokesman admits he doesn't know how many terrorists landed or if all their dinghies have been accounted for.

Amit's mobile phone rings. He drops it, swears, and picks it up again. After several seconds, he lowers it to his side. 'I've been told that late last night two hundred hostages from Australia, Canada, the USA, Israel, France and Germany escaped through hotel windows, using ladders.'

We stare at him, hoping for news of the Holtzbergs.

'No, nothing about Chabad House,' he says in a clipped

voice, as if reading our thoughts. He lowers his eyes to the floor and leans against the doorframe. 'The Indian police won't let us near the place. I feel so helpless, so powerless.'

The television goes blank as he speaks. A siren wails. A picture pops up again – this of a pale baby with a blank look on his face.

'My God, that's Moshe, the Holtzberg's son, and his Indian nanny, Sandra!' The consul flies out of her chair, knocking over a cup of coffee. No one moves. 'On the street near the Jewish House.' A bewildered Sandra stares at the cameras. Perspiration drips from her face onto her shirt. Her hands shake and her lips quiver as she clings to the boy.

'I'm not knowing how I got him out of there,' Sandra pants in stilted English. 'There is so much shouting and shooting.'

Somehow, she'd managed to pick him up off his mother's lifeless chest, run down the stairs, and hide in a stairwell, eventually dashing out the front door, through the gate and into an alley. High-fives echoed across the consul's living room. We crowd closer to the TV set. I run my fingers across the screen as if I'm stroking Sandra's cheek.

'How on earth did Sandra manage to do that?' the Israeli consul murmurs. 'She risked her life for someone else's child.'

I stare at the images of the police and Sandra on the screen and wonder if I could ever find the courage to be so fearless, so selfless.

Day 3: Israeli consul's flat

In the consul's living room, the flat-screen television babbles on continuously amidst the endless comings and goings of Indian officials, security guards and the Israeli ambassador from Delhi. Riveted, we watch repetitive scenes on TV. Especially those of terrorist Ajmal Kasab, caught on CCTV with his AK-47 at the Chhatrapati Shivaji train station.

Chabad House remains under siege. Shots ring out from time to time, but no one knows what's going on inside. Cameras focus on a helicopter flying above the building. Three Indian soldiers cling onto the rope that swings back and forth under the chopper before rappelling onto the flat roof. Far too much time has passed for the Holtzbergs to survive unhurt. We can only hope that they're still alive.

Awful news. Gabi and Rivka have been dead for hours, maybe even days. Anticipating the worst from the outset, the embassy had requested that the *Chevra Kadisha* – a Jewish burial team – be flown in from Israel to prepare the bullet-ridden bodies for burial. They arrive just in time. According to Jewish custom, every shred of flesh and bone has to be carefully collected and buried together, ensuring the ritual cleansing of the body and respect for the dead.

Later that day I meet a young local rabbi, Yitzhak, who'd assisted in the gruesome task. He's suffering from panic attacks after seeing Gabi and Rivka's mutilated bodies in the Chabad building. The consul knows I trained as a psychologist and a trauma therapist during the Yom Kippur War. She asks if I'll talk with him. Fluent in Hebrew, I'm seen as the perfect candidate. But as I try to remember my training from decades earlier, I'm not sure I have the qualifications or expertise.

Rabbi Yitzhak lies face up in the bedroom of one of the consul's kids. His lips quiver and his hands tremble. Ultra-orthodox Jewish protocol forbids any physical contact between men and women, so I sit down cross-legged on the floor next to him. He rolls over on his left side to face me without making eye contact. His face is pale and eyes rimmed in red. Unexpectedly, he thrusts an arm out from under the traditional tasselled prayer shawl and grabs my hand. His fingernails are gnarled and pink.

'Please don't leave me,' Yitzhak pleads in Hebrew and glues his palm onto the back of my hand. Unaccustomed to any physical intimacy in a professional setting, I struggle to throw my awkwardness aside. Staring at the black yarmulke clipped to his hair, I wonder how it must be for him to have me – a woman – as a therapist. But he's too shaken and exhausted to care.

'Please, please stay with me,' he begs again. 'Don't leave me on my own. Every time I close my eyes all I can see are dry brown pools of blood on the floor and bits of skin splattered on the walls.'

His grip tight, Yitzhak pulls me towards him. Trickles of perspiration run down my back. My whole world is upside down. Normally it would be the rabbi's job to counsel the members of his congregation and not the other way round. How can I, a non-believer, be of any real support to a man of God?

He doesn't seem to sense my unease. All the professional trauma counselling skills I learned decades earlier evaporate. He wants more than I'm capable of giving, but I can at least listen to him telling me what he's seen and what he's feeling. One gruesome detail after the other unfolds like the skin from a diseased carcass: Chunks of hair chopped from Gabi's beard lie on the stairs, a discarded Pepsi can dribbled on a mattress near an empty baby's bottle without the teat.

Sweat trickles down the side of Yitzhak's nose as he continues. An endless list of carnage unfolds: A Siddur – a Jewish prayer book – with the pages ripped out, bullet shells, smashed glasses, flies settling on a sneaker soaked in urine, ants crawling on half-eaten sandwiches on the kitchen floor. Wrappers from chocolate wafers covered with blood.

My stomach heaves and I swallow to try to stop myself from vomiting.

Through my blurred atheist lens, I can't see my way to counsel the traumatised young religious leader. After all this, how can he possibly believe in the existence of a God who allows such things to happen? I try to push my own beliefs aside and see his shattered world, but I'm too immersed in his trauma. This struggle to keep my professional distance helps me ignore everything I've learned about PTSD counselling. All I can do is be myself.

I put my free hand on top of Yitzhak's. I want him to know I'm here with him as he tries to come to terms with the murders. He doesn't blink or pull away from this most unorthodox of orthodox behaviour. I realise that solacing his pain is more important than all the religious laws or counselling protocol.

'I can still smell the stench of their putrid flesh,' Yitzhak continues, his body still trembling. 'You are the only person I can tell how scared I feel. No one else will understand that my lungs are still burning from that taste of Hell.' He raises himself on one elbow and continues, 'We found the mangled bodies of four other Israeli visitors on the stairs. Blood everywhere.'

Whatever remaining religious and professional boundaries there may have been between us dissolve as he speaks. Yitzhak's rigid body relaxes. He rolls onto his back, still holding my hand. When he recounts how the terrorists had defecated on the putrefying bodies, I cry and tremble along with him. Nothing has prepared me for this. Not my experiences in the emergency room in Tel Aviv during the Yom Kippur War, nor my work with families who lost loved ones. Not even my own grief as a widow.

This seems to calm him, but my hand won't stop shaking. Finally, when Yitzhak begins to doze off, I uncross my legs. He stirs. Half asleep, he rolls over, increases the pressure of his grip on my hand, and looks to see that I'm still there with him.

Yitzhak helps me realise that compassion knows no boundaries. His religious convictions no longer matter to me. My professional training is of no help. I live with him all the way through his nightmare, giving some comfort to a man whose friends were dismembered, battered and butchered. Yitzhak's sweat mingles with mine, and his stale breath clings to my hair.

When steady, gentle snores fill the room, I stand up and walk down the stairs into the living room. Amit's hand presses up against another security officer's shoulders. Their shirts are creased, beards shadowy and jeans stained.

I bum a cigarette off the policeman guarding the front door and walk out onto the balcony. I haven't smoked for decades, and it tastes foul, but I inhale a couple of deep breaths before I go back in – a futile attempt to calm down and convince myself that we're safe. But deep inside, I know the truth: My world has gone mad.

Every so often, someone pulls me into a corner to talk to me, but I have no advice to give. All I do is listen and recognise how violated and fragile we feel. I wipe away tears, make endless cups of tea and coffee, smear tinned tuna on white bread, top it with mayonnaise, and then slice piles of sandwiches in half.

The consul's three-year-old daughter senses that she's in the middle of a crisis. To calm her, and probably myself, I help her take a bath. The fragrant scent of soap replaces sweat and the suffocating air. It's a relief to be distracted. I wrap her in a soft towel and feel comforted. Isn't it always children who keep the world going round? Or so I think until I'm also asked to meet and counsel the little boy, Moshe, and his nanny, Sandra, who are staying at the flat of the consul's secretary.

Day 4: Home of the Israeli consul's secretary

Moshe, wearing a T-shirt stained with his parents' blood, stands in the corner of a stuffy study. His fists are clenched, his hair matted and his heavy nappy smells of urine. His eyes are dull, lifeless and unfocused, seemingly staring out at another world. A sandwich, a biscuit and a lollipop lie untouched on a small plate near his bare feet. Catatonic, he can't and won't move. Nor does he cry or talk. Sandra, his rescuer, sits on her haunches beside him, gazing at the boy. The baby who heard screams, wails, yells, cries; the baby who smelled blood and gunpowder; the baby who saw terrorists fire guns and hurl hand grenades, who saw his parents collapse and go still. Baby Moshe who has known horror, pain, anguish, shock and trauma. And he's only two years old.

I crouch on the floor next to Sandra and rub her back.

'I don't know myself how I did it.' Sandra grabs my forearm. 'I just did it without thinking. Thanks to God, I got the boy. I only remember running and running and running.

But just look at him. He is so scared from what he saw. Many bad thoughts also wandering constantly through my mind.' Sandra remains squatting as I crouch down next to her. 'This poor boy and his loving mama.'

She reaches out to the toddler and tries to shift Moshe into her lap, but his body is stiff. He cringes when I shift my position a few centimetres to be nearer to him. I pause before slowly backing away.

Forgotten in the chaos, autopsies and death certificates, Sandra clasps my wrists and breathes words I don't understand. But Moshe doesn't forget her. Without warning his legs turn to putty and he falls into her embrace. I want to wrap my arms around them both. Kneeling on the floor next to Sandra, I rub her back as she rocks back and forth.

The consul had asked me to help the family. Even though I wasn't sure there was anything I could do or say, I couldn't refuse. Not after witnessing Sandra's extraordinary feat.

My legs cramp as I wobble to my feet like a ragdoll.

Just then Moshe's grandparents and official guardians arrive from Israel to collect their children for burial in the Holy Land. The couple, eyes swollen, sink into a sofa in the living room, oblivious to the security agents and embassy staff milling around us. The rabbi tugs at his beard and stares into his lap. He doesn't try to stop his yarmulke sliding off his balding head. Yehudit's crumpled black skirt reached down to the floor, and she clutches a tissue in her clenched fist. She moves one forearm to dab her eyes and blow her nose, as if she's a robot acting on instructions. One foot jitters, and her heel taps the floor in an uneven rhythm. She stretches out her calf and pulls it in, and the tremors start again.

When I suggest they try to play with Moshe, they stare at me, *through* me, as if I'm not really here. I ache to fill their hearts with some warmth. They probably sense that I can't identify with their religious claim that 'It was all God's will'. I want them to be here, with and for their grandson. To sit on the floor with Moshe, talk to him, read him a story and coax him to eat and drink. A sandwich, a biscuit, yogurt, some ice cream. While I focus on Moshe's welfare, my attention to their agony dwindles. Their tragedy. Their loss. Their children's suffering before they died. All I can think of is the toddler.

Sitting on a chair facing them, I put my hands under my thighs so no one can see them shaking. When I ask them if they will come and play with Moshe, they stare at me as if I'm crazy.

'We're too old,' they say in unison, as if chanting a prayer. Looking at their slumped shoulders, dull expressions and calcified wrinkles, I can believe them. They tell me they're too exhausted and old to care for Moshe at home. A boarding school run by the Chabad community is the solution to his wellbeing. For his own good.

The air-conditioner drones on, and mobiles ring. Someone must've placed a mug of black Nescafé in my hands because I remember tasting the sweet, warm liquid. A cheese sandwich wrapped in a paper napkin lands in my lap. I take a bite but can't swallow. The soft white bread sticks to the roof of my mouth.

Looking over at Moshe sleeping in Sandra's lap as she sits cross-legged on the floor leaning against a wall, I shake my head. He's all I care about. A jumble of syllables shuffles around my brain.

'Sandra should come back with you and help you take care of him,' I hear myself say, a little too loudly. My eyes don't flicker – I look straight at them. 'She says she wants to stay with him.'

It's unusual for me to be so insistent. Words that aren't mine seem to come from someone else. When Rabbi Shimon grunts and stands up, my dogmatic voice softens to a murmur. Sweat channels down the deep wrinkles in his face and into his beard. He looks at the catatonic boy and sits down again, with a long, sustained moan. Yehudit sniffles, looking down at the floor and shaking her head.

My chair falls over as I stand, but I leave it lying there as I rush to the bathroom. I turn on the tap to drown out the sound of retching, splash cold water on my face, rinse out my mouth and spit into the basin. I'm totally out of my depth. I realise I'm too harsh on Moshe's grandparents. They have to come to terms with the murder of their son and daughter-in-law, five months' pregnant, as well as to care for a grandson they barely know. Perhaps they're left with little energy to try to play with Moshe, feed him, change him and comfort him.

When I come back, Rabbi Shimon looks at me and nods.

The air-conditioner drones on, starting and stopping as the air pulsates into the room. Eyelids droop. Chatter ceases. Hours of non-stop listening spur me on to find that extra emotional strength to deal with all the surrounding pain and tragedy. Strength that drifted away from me when John died returns. Now I connect with a renewed sense of purpose and identity. A quest to find out why. Why me? Why us?

While Moshe and Sandra remain the focus of our attention, the news channels bombard us with grim facts. More than one hundred and sixty-eight innocent people killed. Hundreds maimed, hospitalised and unaccounted for. '*Mumbaikers*' become one big family obsessed with sharing what we've been through. A kind of group therapy. Everyone knows someone who is a victim. We learn a few days later that nine of the terrorists associated with the Pakistani terror group were killed.

After a few weeks, we may sleep a little better, have fewer nightmares and return to work. But not to normal.

Security cameras captured a video of the lone survivor, Kasab, striding through Mumbai's main railway station with his AK-47 assault rifle and a rucksack crammed with ammunition. For days after his capture, the BBC, CNN and Asian TV stations share that enduring image.

Day 5: Mumbai synagogue

The memorial service for Gabi and Rivka is being held at Mumbai's Magen David Synagogu. I squeeze into a row packed with dignitaries and everyday people – Muslims and Christians as well as Jews. Rabbis, imams, priests, businessmen, schoolchildren, cleaners, shop owners, teachers, ambassadors, waiters, soldiers, nurses, doctors, photographers and journalists. All suffered losses; all show up to grieve.

Towards the end of the service, Moshe starts calling for his mother. In the arms of the late couple's cook, he wriggles and screams, 'Ima, Ima, Ima' – the Hebrew for mother. His cries lacerate my heart. Sandra, who must still complete the formalities for her Israeli tourist visa application, isn't here to comfort him. Inconsolable, his anguish rises to the top of the high domed ceiling, clinging to the blue-and-red stained-glass windows. I can't stop sobbing. Even the men wipe their eyes. It's impossible to conceive that our God is listening.

The following day I meet the family for the last time as they depart for the airport. Sandra leaves her adult sons behind to live in a strange land with a strange language, strange food, strange dress and unfamiliar culture. Her only luggage consists of a small plastic bag with a shirt, trousers, pair of trainers, hairbrush, flip-flops and toothbrush.

A few days later, Rivka and Gabi and their unborn child are buried on the Mount of Olives in Jerusalem. Rabbi Yitzhak stays on in Mumbai, and we have several therapy sessions together. I'm the only outlet he has for his anguish. Newlywed, he's deeply concerned for his wife who's four months' pregnant. He can't stop looking over his shoulder.

'With my black coat and black hat, I'm an obvious target,' he says. 'I keep waiting for another attack.' I can't stop seeing what he's seen, smelling the stench in Chabad House and feeling a collective vulnerability.

Life seems to return to normal, but we stare at strangers suspiciously. Hotels put up barricades and search vehicles and guests' bags. Security checks are the new norm at airports, cinemas, concerts, supermarkets and restaurants. It takes two weeks to get a new mobile phone. The government institutes police checks for foreigners like me before we can have a SIM card.

At work, all we can talk about is India's 9/11. We sit for hours every day glued to the television, watching the same scenes over and over again. Kasab firing at commuters, smoke spewing out the Taj Mahal Palace Hotels, bodies lying in the streets. There's no financial or emotional government support for locals who lost breadwinners or limbs. The psychological scars are raw.

* * *

Images of Moshe's empty eyes appear when I shower, when I eat, when I walk up the stairs to my office. When I close my eyes I search for my own grandchildren's radiant chocolate and saucer-blue eyes. Sometimes it's a struggle to find them. Even though I haven't been shot at or jumped out of a window, I lie awake at night staring at the spinning ceiling fan turning, hoping it will lull me to sleep. As I toss and turn, drenched with perspiration, a vibrant culture once filled with energy, colour, beauty and warmth transforms into a land of sorrow and bewilderment. All that seems to matter now is hugging my own family.

Moshe's vacant eyes, wails of despair and rigid body shake my belief that India might become my home for at least a few more years. Shortly after the attack, I plan to move once again, and this time to become an integral part of my own family's daily lives.

In the midst of the horror, I realise that my company's market price, profit margins and overall strategic direction are irrelevant. Yet a silent bond of shared traumatic experience binds me to my colleagues. I can't leave them in the lurch. But I also need to prepare myself for yet another move to another completely different city, Seattle, where my daughter and her family live.

Sandra remains in Israel where she's named an honorary

citizen in recognition of her extraordinary courage. She works at an institution for physically and emotionally challenged children and visits Moshe on weekends. I often think of her and wonder what she'll do when Moshe is older. She remains an inspiration and a role model for me. I hardly know her, but she's selfless. She gave up so much to stand for what she believes: in devotion, loyalty and love.

Five days before the fourth anniversary of the 2008 Mumbai terror attacks, the lone captured terrorist, Kasab, hangs for his role in the carnage. With the long drawn-out trial finally over, I hope the families and friends of the victims will enjoy some closure. When I shut my eyes, I can still see the blue wall in baby Moshe's bedroom where his parents marked several little pencil lines as he grew. Thankfully, living with his grandparents in the north of Israel, he will continue to grow.

The Chabad community from around the world finances the rebuilding of the destroyed centre in Mumbai. It won't be completed for six long years. But, when the centre re-opens, it will be a beacon of light in the darkness, its people sharing the unshakeable belief that good always triumphs over evil.

The massacre in Mumbai and my conversations with Yitzhak shatter my idea that there might be a safe home – anywhere. I come to grips with the concept of universal trauma. What happened in Mumbai could happen anywhere to anyone. But there is life afterward – even if it veers off at a completely different angle.

It will be another year before I leave Mumbai. But even then, I know that Mumbai will never leave me.

HOPE

CHAPTER 14

A New Man in My Life

On the eve of the Muslim festival Eid al-Adha, herds of goats en route to slaughter clog every intersection in Mumbai. Every time a herdsman's stick or an animal's shank bangs into my car I flinch, sigh and swear. Occasionally, Khamat unscrews the cap off a plastic water bottle and takes a few sips. I sit, newspaper folded, trying to be patient. It doesn't help that I'm struggling with today's *Times of India* crossword

'It's okay,' he says as he turns to look at me. 'Soon you will be home.'

I shrug and smile back. 'You're right.'

'Tonight is the big celebration for the Muslims,' Khamat explains, looking at me in the rearview mirror, trying to temper my irritation. 'They will start the festival by killing the goats and having a big feast. You are knowing, *merrim,* that we Hindus, we are only eating veg. Today, Abdul from Security, he is telling me the story about this holiday. You see, his god was telling Abraham to sacrifice his son, Ismael. But when he tried to do this, he found he had killed the goat.'

Determined to be my teacher while I'm in India, Khamat is more than my driver. He's an important figure in my life.

I spend four, sometimes five hours a day with my protector, mentor and informant. Sometimes he shares the company gossip from other drivers: Who fights with his wife, who goes clubbing until after midnight and who has another job offer.

'Tonight is a bad traffic night. Much slow.' Khamat grimaces as he looks around. 'Now I make a detour on the airport road. Don't worry.'

I worry. As he shifts onto a narrow lane on the highway, he checks his rearview mirror and turns against the oncoming traffic down the shoulder of the Airoli Bridge. He revs the accelerator as if we're about to be the first to cross the finish line in the Indian Grand Prix.

I instinctively duck. My neck cricks. My fingers grip the door handle.

A few seconds later, when I dare to raise my head, I see a narrow lane under the highway stretching out before us. We survived the detour and now the traffic is actually flowing with us rather than against us.

By the time I arrive home, my hair is matted. My head throbs and my mood is dark.

I unlock my front door, kick off my flip-flops and walk into the living room. And *freeze*.

Someone has been here, in my flat! I can sense it, I can *smell* it, and I can't move. My experience with an intruder on the first night in my Mumbai flat keeps my antennae on high alert.

In my flat I shift my eyes and, without moving my head, stare into the living room. The chairs and table are in their usual place and my iPad is right where I left it this morning.

The television and remote are on the bookcase. Everything looks fine, but something is wrong. *Something.*

It's the smell. Not the smell of freshly washed floors or the steamy sea breeze that typically greets me at night. Traces of sandalwood perhaps? Or maybe Brylcreem?

Yes, that's it. The faint trail of a male presence. Beads of perspiration roll down the back of my neck. I close my eyes, open them, close them again and pause. What will I do if I come face to face with a thief?

Holding my breath, I peer around the corner into the kitchenette.

Nothing.

I clench my jaw and back up against the wall, feeling my way police-style, like they do in the movies. I grip my front door key firmly between the second and third fingers of my right hand and clench my fist. I'm ready to gouge out the eye of any unwelcome visitor. Ready to back out the front door. Ready to run. To scream. Whatever works.

Wait. Is this really happening? Again? Or am I fantasising? Has the worse-than-usual traffic, the bleating goats and incessant honking, made me paranoid?

Then I remember. It's Tuesday night. My cook, Radha – the new man in my life – must have come earlier to cook my dinner. His lingering smell hangs in the living room. Slowly I ease into the small passage. The aroma of garlic, coriander, lemon and harissa wafts from the kitchen. I put my briefcase and laptop down on the coffee table and take a deep breath before turning on the tap to wash my hands.

At the table, I lift a sheet of aluminium foil off a plate to find a mini-banquet of fresh chapatti, masala potatoes, bitter gourd with chopped carrots, and curried cauliflower. It's magic to my hungry eyes. *Heaven.* My mouth tingles. *Ahh…Radha!*

The stone floor cools the soles of my feet as I raise an imaginary glass to symbolically toast my neighbour, Rushina, the owner of the flat I rent. She insisted on introducing me to her cook. The vegetarian kedgeree, chickpeas in curry sauce, and cottage cheese cubes in spinach gravy that I enjoyed on the numerous occasions I dined at her home are a testament to her recommendation.

'You must only eat the best of Indian foods while in Mumbai,' Rushina said, waving her finger at me. 'It's not enough that you're eating cafeteria food of rice, dal and curd for lunch, and only salad for dinner.' She twisted her magenta scarf over her back. 'I will make sure you have the best cook, and a very nice dinner a couple of evenings every week,' she said patting my cheek. 'Radha cooks for many families in our block of flats. Every morning he is going to the market,' she said, lifting her arms to kiss her fingertips. 'He is buying fresh garlic, parsley, tomatoes, onions and carrots. He makes sure he selects only the good vegetables. You'll see, you'll be having a better dinner than your queen in Buckingham Palace.'

When I finally met Radha for the first time, I understood why he's so popular. It may be the food, but the truth is, he's also drop-dead gorgeous. There's no other way to describe the way his eyes crinkle, his firm and reserved way of speaking and the manner in which he folds his arms across his chest like an Indian prince about to bark out his royal commands.

He twirls his moustache as if he's Omar Sharif meeting Lawrence of Arabia at the well. A mirage in my desert, he stands at least six feet tall and carries the form of an athlete – sinewy, muscular and erect. He smells of eucalyptus, sandalwood and rosemary. Everything he cooks has a Michelin star.

On our first meeting, Radha entered my kitchen and clenched his jaw. He sniffed and looked down at me. I crumbled beneath his gaze. He was unimpressed.

'*Merrim*, this is no Indian kitchen! Where is the spatula, the chapatti pan? Nothing to grind the spices. Why no cloves, no fenugreek, no turmeric? Where is the pots, how are you wanting me to cook?'

I blushed, and I don't blush easily. Was that how Lawrence felt when he met Sharif at the well? When the Bedouin sultan with the romantic eyes replied, 'My name is for my friends?'

I was unsure what to say or do. Radha stormed out my front door and into the corridor. He rapped on Rushina's door.

'*Merrim!*' he cried, gesticulating wildly as she stepped out. He burst into a torrent of Hindi, beyond anything I could possibly comprehend. But the gist was clear.

After he finished, Rushina looked past him to where I stood frozen in my doorway. The frown disappeared from her forehead as she came up to me.

'Do not worry. Saturday, I take you shopping,' she said. 'We go to the kitchen market and buy you some things so that Radha can start to cook for you next week. Please, you mustn't worry.'

Rushina turned to Radha and waved him off, speaking gently yet firmly. His grimace vanished. All I understood of what she said was chapatti, pepper, garlic and grinder.

Radha faced me and nodded. '*Aacha*, yes, Tuesday,' he confirmed, slapping a fly away from his neck. 'Nay too much spicy.' He touched me on my elbow and strode off towards the exit. His sandals plopped against the concrete as he sprinted down two steps at a time.

On the morning of our shopping expedition, Rushina, resplendent in a floral maroon-and-lime sari, gripped my elbow as we spilled out of the three-wheeler rickshaw into a market lane. Tiny stores overflowed with pots and pans – copper, aluminium and clay. Finjan coffee pots, big round spice trays, wooden chapatti boards, copper bowls or *katoris*, mortars and pestles and rolling pins filled the shelves and carpeted the concrete floors. Of the hundreds of shops to choose from, how did Rushina know which ones to visit? To me, all stores look the same. To Rushina, there are only two or three worth visiting.

'This one here has the freshest spices,' she said. 'Here we buy the griddle, and this one, the pots.' Rushina gathered her sari off the floor with one hand, draped the fabric around her elbow, and began bargaining with the shopkeepers. She turned to me, whispering. 'You must never pay what they are asking. They are expecting to bargain. Especially for you, a foreigner, they will push up the prices.'

I looked around again at the endless kitchenware in that Aladdin's cave, and Rushina laughed at the expression on my face.

'Your eyes are about to pop out of your head. And shut your mouth before you swallow a fly!'

Shoppers with sharp elbows bulled through a lane of cooking utensils, pushing, shoving and bumping. I wanted to take in every smell possible. I wanted to recall the colours and shapes of every utensil and relish the energy and vitality bursting out around me so I could bottle them and pull out the cork whenever I felt the need.

Hours later, we overloaded a rickshaw with everything a kitchen might need. The vehicle sagged and swayed as we began the journey back home. Our shopping bags scraped the sandy streets. We ran over a pothole and everything clanged together as if we were cymbals in a concerto.

'Hang in there.' Rushina put her arm around my shoulder to keep me from falling out. I hadn't yet perfected the locals' knack for maintaining my balance as we swayed, thumped and wobbled our way down the street.

A few days later, I decide the time is right to share my new lifestyle in an email to my kids, describing how wonderful it is to come home, put my feet up on the grid of my small balcony, wrap fresh chapattis around potatoes with mint chutney, crunch on fried okra and savour mixed vegetable sambar – a soup made with lentils, roasted spices and fresh coconut. I describe each mouthful as I listen to the waves breaking on the rocks below. I write,

My taste buds seem to have risen from the dead. Radha is so important in my life…

But my kids only read the subject line: 'There is a new man in my life' along with the first paragraph describing the dishes Radha prepares. How his evening meals make me forget my long rides home and busy days at the office.

If they had read on, they would have understood that I hardly ever see him, that we don't text or speak by phone. That I leave cash for him every week, but come home far too late to see or thank him personally.

Instead, I receive a series of urgent calls from home. 'Mum, is this a good idea? Isn't it too soon? Who is this guy? What do you know about him? Can he teach you how to cook so you can prepare Indian meals for us?'

One morning on the way to work I met Radha running up the stairs. He held out a bunch of celery, crushed its leaves and lifted the stalks to my nose.

'I buy this fresh now, you can tell. It's smelling so good.'

I smiled and bobbed my head. I'd never been a fan of celery before, but from that moment on, I was intoxicated. Now, I snack on it often.

With the passage of time in Mumbai, I find myself becoming an adventurous eater; exposing my palate to an array of different delicacies. I always try them – curry leaves, turmeric, bitter gourd, okra, snake gourd – even if I don't like them.

There are still times, especially in those early morning hours, when I fret over what I've lost and what I've given up. These regrets are less frequent. Now, when my green parrot perches on my kitchen ledge at the same time every morning, I believe it's a positive omen. I name him Kumar, after the handsome male character in the *Jewel of the Crown*. Not once does Kumar peck at the chopped peppers or mango in the saucer I leave for him, but he stays for several minutes, each time cocking his head to one side and staring at me. It seems as if all he wants to do is look into my eyes.

Maybe he's the new influence in my life I should have shared with my kids. Maybe they would have understood that a little better.

I crane my head to mimic him as I attempt to stare Kumar down. He seems to know we're playing a game.

CHAPTER 15

Sense and Sensuality

The hotel lift rattles its way up to the sixth floor. I grab the handle of the iron gate and slide it open. Even before we step out, the sounds of bongo drums and guitars echo down the corridor. A sour odour wafts along the passage. Not stale air. Not mould. Slightly peppery.

Gita walks ahead of me, her sepia-coloured sari trailing after her. 'Now the wedding ceremonies are beginning.' She throws her head back and laughs. 'You're in for a big treat.' She strides ahead, oblivious to the fact that the noise is drowning out her voice. I walk faster, trying to catch what she's saying. 'We go to the ceremony for the groom. His father is my cousin. Or rather my mother's cousin.' Gita picks up the pace as if rushing to catch a train, her dupatta floating behind her. 'At the bride's house is a party for the bride now. For her relatives.'

She pushes on a half-open door to the hotel suite. The bass grows louder. We slip off our sandals. The music vibrates right through me. The soles of my feet tingle.

After hugging a couple I assume are her relatives, Gita introduces me. 'This is my friend Sue, from the UK.' She gently nudges me forward. I nod and smile and say namaste, pressing my palms together at my chest. Even though they both carry on talking while looking at me, I can hear nothing more than, 'Velcome, velcome. We are so happy you can come to our son's wedding.'

The room, a little larger than a table tennis table, overflows with men, women, teens and kids – the groom's relatives – aunties, uncles, cousins and grandparents. All wear shades of yellow: mustard and pumpkin-coloured tunics; saffron and orange pantaloons; mandarin and gold saris. All talk loudly to make themselves heard above the music. My black-and-white cotton patterned kurta and trousers, the outfit that I bought especially for the occasion, is totally out of place. *If only I'd asked someone.* A pale foreigner wearing even paler clothes, I'm an outsider, alone and apprehensive. Children stare – and some of the women, too – at my white skin and my greying hair.

The groom, Ashish, wears an ochre silk kurta and sits grinning, cross-legged on a pile of scarlet cushions with gold tassels. The disco music with its distinct Bollywood twang gets softer as we all sit down on the carpeted floor. Legs crossed, legs to the side, legs under.

Shadows shift across the ceiling. Someone draws the floral curtains to shut out the afternoon sun. The air-conditioner drones on, straining beneath the heavy load of a roomful of sweating people. Children giggle. Women whisper and men fidget with their sherwanis; long coat-like tops, pulling them across their knees so that they don't crease.

Without warning, the bridegroom's parents leap up off the paisley carpet and rush up to their son. They rip the silk shirt from his back. Laughter, cheering and whistles mingle together as someone holds up a large plastic bowl. One by one, the guests dip their hands into an orange, muddy concoction so much like sticky peanut butter and smear it across Ashish's back. They plaster his neck, chest and cheeks, hair and forehead. The same pungent, biting aroma that filled the corridor overwhelms the room.

After only a month in India, I'm already attending my first wedding celebration. The movie *Monsoon Wedding* painted a picture of what to expect with Bollywood dancing; long, lust-filled glances and complicated religious rituals. But nothing had prepared me for the frenetic intimacy of the *Haldi*. Pulsating rhythms mix with shrill laughter and echo around the room. But the laughter is not mine. Suddenly it reminds me of just how alone and abandoned I feel. My fists tighten into a ball.

As the rest of the guests join in the scrum, scooping the muddy sludge from the bowl and smearing it over the groom, I glance around and fold my arms. My feet shuffle backward as I wonder, *What next?* Whatever it is, I know I'm not ready for it.

I scour the room for an escape route, inching my way towards a nearby wall, hoping no one notices as I take refuge behind the billowing curtains near the sputtering air-conditioner. Suddenly, someone calls out.

'Susan! C'mon. Don't be so serious.'

I look up and force a smile. It's Gita. *Cornered. Caught. Captured.* She's right. I *am* serious. I realise all at once just *how* serious. How it still hurts to laugh, and how my smiles feel false. At home, my bedside table sags beneath the weight of my 'serious' literature – *The Rise and Fall of the Third Reich*, *The True Story of Lawrence of Arabia* and back issues of *The Economist*. To add to my misery and shame, a well of envy washes over me.

Envy for all the other people in the room enjoying everything I once had and lost – kisses, hugs and the companionship of a beloved soulmate. Why should they have so much fun when I'm still so melancholy? I feel as if my life is over.

Involuntarily, I lift my wedding ring to my lips and kiss it.

Gita had insisted I join her at a relative's wedding in Nagda, an hour-and-a-half flight from Mumbai.

'You don't know India until you've been a wedding guest,' she said, her voice insistent. 'It doesn't matter that you don't know the family. They are my cousins and will be very happy to have you, my new friend, as their guest.' She put a firm hand on my shoulder as if to convince me. 'This is India,' Gita says, shaking her head, 'we're always inviting guests.'

Now, draped in orange silks and a sparkling emerald necklace, Gita swirls around. Rays of sunshine stream through the wall of windows behind her, illuminating her jet-black hair.

'Rubbing his body with this paste is propitious!' she shouts. 'Turmeric is a very auspicious spice. It's also antiseptic. It's a symbolic cleansing of the body and the soul to ensure the groom has a long and happy married life.'

Placing a squishy blob of the elixir into the palm of my hand, she leads me to the small group of family members whom I'd met only that day. 'You have to rub some paste on Ashish's back.'

I lift my hand and take a deep breath. It's the turmeric! That's the mystery aroma. I flip my hair behind my ears with my free hand and take a step forward.

'We are asking the holy spirits to bless the couple-to-be and protect them from evil spirits,' Gita says. 'The bride, Sunita, is having a ceremony of her own with her relatives.'

Since I'm unfamiliar with the protocol, my only option is to follow everyone else. Letting down my guard, I slide my palm across Ashish's muscular back. Sensuous memories rush in as I feel his smooth skin tensing beneath my fingers. Rubbing the shoulders of a stranger feels both intimate and uncomfortable. My body tingles from the contact rekindling my dormant sensuality. I thought I had lost it for ever.

John and I enjoyed a playful relationship. I loved running my fingers up and down his back. How I wish I was caressing him now. I close my eyes and imagine the touch of his skin. And I hear him whisper and think to myself, *Yes. Oh, yes. I hear you.*

'You have to stop pining for me,' the voice says. 'Go ahead and have some fun. Go on.' John nudges me forward. But how can I enjoy myself without him?

When Gita pulls me into the circle of dancers, John's large hands hold onto mine. His baritone voice sings along with the men cheering me on.

Voluptuous plump midriffs peek at me through alluring, wispy cloth. Gold bangles jingle as the women twirl their wrists in circles above their heads. Buxom cleavages and flabby arms mingle seductively. At first, I envy the sensuous saris and jiggling movements of the women. Then, even though wrists, my hands and feet are the only visible parts of my body, here I am – Madam Conservative – just fitting right in. For the first time since John's death my head, if not my heart, is ready to play. I wonder who I really am – the laughing, dancing free spirit I'd once been or the pale, serious widow I find myself to be here in India, shrinking away from life?

Twelve years earlier at my hen party in a Soho bar in

London, a handsome stranger invited me to tango. I spun around, wearing an organza veil decorated with condoms as tassels. There was so much to look forward to then. Can I revive my deadened self?

Drawing me out of my reverie, Shipali, Ashish's mother, throws an orange pashmina over my shoulders. The soft fabric brushes my cheek as she giggles. 'We will turn you into an Indian princess yet.' She squeals as her strong arms whirl me around.

Struggling to keep my balance, I focus on a splendour of riches spread out on the bedcover in the corner of the suite. Saris and jewellery fill several large baskets wrapped in cellophane and tied with billowy red bows. A diamond necklace lies on deep-magenta silk, and chains of gold drape themselves atop aquamarine organza. Women in India, not only the rich ones, collect expensive jewels, which provide them with financial security should something happen to their husbands or family.

Gita tugs my arm harder, and, when I don't move, she tries to pull me in again. I slide out of my fog into a treasure trove of laughter.

'Those are presents for the bride and her mother,' Gita says, her eyes following mine. 'You remember I did tell you about Indian weddings. The ceremonies, the colours, the joy. But I don't think you quite believed that it would be so very different from your weddings there in London.' She throws her arms around me. 'You'll get used to our wonderful country so very soon. Soon you'll be laughing again.'

I wonder how Gita knows that my first wedding here in India will be the starting block to get me back on track. Or if she just intuitively realises that I lost my sense of self when my husband died – that curious, spontaneous, adventurous woman that John had called his bobby dazzler. Lancashire jargon for someone who's done something great and funny. It isn't as if I don't know *how* to return to the real world. The 'doing it' is the problem.

That night I dream of a volcano spitting out black ash all over me. I start to run away to escape the terror of being smothered. My feet stick in the mud sliding down the mountainside. And then a gust of wind blows from another direction. The volcanic ash turns scarlet and spews out dancing papayas and laughing mangoes. Sweet and juicy. I leap into the air to try to catch them, but they keep slipping through my ashen fingers.

When I wake in the early hours of the morning, I roll over and shake my arms, blowing the volcanic powder off me. I look around the room, blink several times and check my wristwatch. *Just what I thought,* I say to myself. *I've wasted too much time feeling sorry for myself already. Now it's time for me to get a new outlook on life.*

That morning, before the wedding ceremony, I resolve to brighten my sombre attire. The leap from serious, West End chic to Bollywood glamour is an Olympic long jump, but I have to give it a try. The physical transformation from colourless to glamorous may be just the catalyst I need for an emotional charge. My hair, limp from humidity and heat, plus a clenched jaw and black-and-white cotton shalwar kameez have to go. But simply adorning myself in a silk sari may make me look like an even greater misfit. Still, I resolve, I have to try.

While Gita helps Shipali pin her sari, I pluck up enough courage to take the elevator to the reception, walk through the lobby and out into the sunlit street and into the bustling local market. On my own. Nagda's vendors speak little English, but a few smiles, lots of hand movements and laughter overcome all barriers. Peering into a hand mirror tied onto the curtain of one of the small shacks, I try on a pair of dazzling four-inch imitation diamond drop earrings that shimmer and tinkle when I shake my head. Quite different from the tiny pearl studs I usually wear. Glitzy gold stiletto sandals adorned with lime-green plastic stars replace my black flats.

Behind a curtain, a woman shows me how to wear an apricot and sky-blue sari for that evening's reception. But as a first step into my new world, I start with something a bit less flashy. I choose a sequined kurta with matching pantaloons.

'Ma'am, pretty, pretty now,' the woman says as she clasps an imitation ruby necklace behind my neck and giggles. I step back, and she nods approvingly. With a rainbow of plastic bangles from my wrists to my elbows, I'm off to the next shack.

A few stalls down at the edge of the road I find a manicure parlour where I sit on a blue plastic bucket. Not long after, I hold my hands up, my finger and toenails glistening crimson in the sun. Next I sit on a three-legged stool on the pavement as a hair stylist insists on colouring my roots blonde-brown. An hour later I look younger and stand straighter. Even though my anxious spirit still huddles in the shadows, the rest of me feels ready to party. I look the part too, even if only cosmetically.

The camouflage works better than I could have imagined. The hotel receptionist who'd drawn me a sketch of where to go shopping earlier that morning, doesn't recognise me when I ask for the room key.

'Sorry, madam,' she says, frowning, 'but there is a private

event at this hotel and that room is occupied. You must be mistaken.'

When I tell her my name her cheeks flush and she looks down at the floor. 'I'm so sorry,' she says, 'but when you left this morning you wore different clothes, and your hair was mostly grey.'

'Yes, I did some shopping and went to the hair salon you recommended. Thanks for your advice.'

Back in our hotel room Gita looks at me, blinks and takes a step back.

'*Wow*, you look so different.' She laughs and covers her mouth with her hands. '*Wow*. Now, for certain, you definitely belong here in India!'

I run my fingers through my hair to show off my new earrings and she nods her approval.

'And that sequined mauve kurta lifts your skin tones and complements your new hair,' she says, stopping to pin her sari. 'I really like your new look. It makes you look so elegant!'

Gita, on the other hand, looks like a maharani with her long black hair tucked behind her ears and nestling across her shoulders. Bronze blush exaggerates her high cheekbones, and her full lips shine with brilliant coral paint. Cobalt-blue eye shadow highlights her brown eyes, clearly defined by the thick eyeliner and mascara.

An authentic ruby necklace with four large stones nestles in the cleft of her large bosom. Long gold drop earrings sway side to side as she sprays her underarms with rose perfume. The soft silk fabric draped around her back exposes plump rolls around her midriff. Although I envy her seductive attire, the thought of taking an even bigger step into Indian fashion fills me with dread. Clumsy me, I imagine my sari unravelling all around me because I haven't pinned it properly. *No*, I think. *Don't panic. Baby steps. Baby steps.*

'You hear those trumpets?' Gita says suddenly, taking my arm. 'We must hurry now to accompany the groom to the bride's home.'

A red carpet with no end in sight rolls out from the hotel entrance. When the groom, wearing a white turban and long silk jacket, appears on a white horse, four musicians, wearing black trousers and silver shirts, lift their parade drums, strap them to their waists, and roll their drumsticks. We're about to begin our journey on foot. Four more musicians raise their trumpets to blast out a rhythmic tune as we clap and whistle along with the other guests. The scent of sandalwood mixes with the heat and dust of the day, clinging to my senses like a honey bear to a hive. Dazzling colours and sweaty bodies whisk me into another world where dreams of those delectable papayas and juicy mangoes are almost in reach.

Red carpet. White horse. Trumpets. Drums.

The scene makes Disney's take on Cinderella's ball look tame. Living in a fairy tale, I hope the horse won't poop as we follow the crowd. Walking next to me, Anu, the groom's sister wears a sari made of gold thread that twinkles as she walks.

'It was my wedding dress last year,' she whispers in my ear. She lets out a breath and wipes the back of her hand across her brow. '*Wow*. It is like a furnace in here.'

Knowing that Anu is also uncomfortable takes some of the sting out of my new sandals, which already feel a size too small as my feet swell in the heat. I don't even mind the perspiration pooling at the back of my neck. Hands grab hands and palms are sweaty. Emeralds, diamonds, rubies, gold necklaces and bracelets gleam against flesh and fabric. Men in Nehru black silk embroidered jackets and long bright-pink scarves whistle and cheer, to the sound of boisterous rhythms.

It's been a while since I counted laughter and joy among my two closest friends. *I'm not used to this.* Forgetting where I am, I snap back in time and look around for John to join the fun – but he's nowhere to be seen. For a few seconds my glitzy adornments torment me. Then the incessant pulse of the music grabs hold, and I'm back in the moment – back in India – again.

Greeted by the bride's parents, we enter a large garden surrounded by eucalyptus trees and the wedding ceremony begins. A priest in a white sarong, with a long grey beard down to his chest, chants prayers on a ceremonial stage while he holds his hands over a small fire. The bridal couple sit opposite each other. The bride, wearing a scarlet sari with gold embroidery stares at the floor, coyly avoiding eye contact with her intended. Her diamond nose stud glistens in the afternoon sun. Gold bangles adorn her arms from her wrists to her elbows. Family members walk on and off the stage, blessing the couple.

The groom looks serious and somewhat forlorn. I can't help but wonder if he'd known his betrothed before. Even though 'love marriages' are now more common in India, the time from engagement to wedding can often be as short as a few weeks rather than months or years.

My civil wedding with John at London's Finsbury Town Hall was quite a different affair. Built in the 1890s, the hall was adorned with baroque female figures, carved friezes and stained-glass windows. I wore a fitted maroon-brown suit with a silk collar and a pair of pearl earrings that John had given me as a wedding gift. We held hands and smiled at one another when the registrar asked us to repeat the marriage vows. Our audience of thirty guests laughed when, in all the excitement, I stumbled over John's middle name, Donald. Wedding rings on our fingers, we raised our hands joined as one as the audience clapped. It was so much fun and all over in fifteen minutes.

Here in Nagda, this wedding is a three-day shebang. As the sun slips lower in the sky, I look out over a sea of faces. Nearly a thousand guests are seated for dinner in the sprawling garden. Glistening candles lend a fairy-tale effect to the scene. A banquet buffet of silver platters adorns crisp white cloths on long trestle tables. Spicy paneer, Indian-style cheese, melts in my mouth. I mop up the curried beans with garlic naan bread and take a second helping of potatoes fried with mustard seeds. My palate tingles with excitement over each new flavour.

Eucalyptus trees form a barrier between the kitchens and the dance floor. I pick a leaf, crush it in my palm and take a deep breath. The strong scent clears my head of any doubts that I have that I am finally *moving on*, even though my *mourning* sickness still manages to tug me back down. Like when Vijay, the groom's uncle, a tall man with a mischievous smile and handlebar moustache, finds me skulking near an oleander bush. *All I want to do is fade into the background again.*

'Please, Miss Sue, it is too nice a night. Come. Dance with me.' Vijay reaches out his slender fingers. I want to say no. No thanks. For a moment I flash back to when John and I danced at the Savoy Hotel in London. In between cucumber sandwiches, cream scones and shortbread served on a silver cake stand, we performed our best Fred and Ginger, laughing as we tried not to trip over our own feet. Now, the thought of dancing with another man is agonising. *I only want to dance with John. I don't want to hold another man's hand or come close enough to smell his body scent. But it would be rude to refuse.*

As we walk across the grass, one heel of my new stilettos sinks into the ground, and my ankle collapses. I stumble onto the wooden dance platform and into Vijay's arms. My new bangles jangle a little too loudly, and my cheeks burn a little too much. Vijay takes my forearm to steady me.

'Goodness me,' he says, as he helps me regain my balance. 'Why don't you take off those ridiculous sandals? You have such pretty feet.'

He smiles, nodding at me as I hesitate only briefly before reaching down and flinging the stilettos onto the grass. I'm surprised to see him staring at my toes. I have slim ankles and a high arch, it's true. But who ever noticed them before? I look down at my feet through his eyes and see what he sees – ten crimson toenails glistening in the moonlight,

Vijay starts to shuffle to the music, slowly at first. He takes a kerchief from his pocket and whirls it around my head. Shoulders shimmy and hips sway to the rhythm of the Bollywood hit song, It's Rocking. His hips, and then mine.

A ring of people surrounds us chanting, 'Susan, Susan!' Now we're centre stage.

Bangles tinkle as I twirl around. I let out a *whoop*. And another. And still more until my voice turns hoarse. We dance late into the evening until it's time for me to return to my hotel room. As, as I settle into the soft coolnesss of the crisp white bed linens, I think about all that had happened that day. About the plethora of sights and sounds and scents washing over me from earliest morning to late at night.

Turmeric.

I wonder about the magical essence of the spice and how it contributed to my reawakening this weekend. And I wonder if, whenever I smell its aroma, I'll look back upon this wedding night as an epic event. Not only for the young marrieds, but also for me. It proved to be my Indian 'coming out' party when the winds of change reached out and grabbed me by the hand.

CHAPTER 16

Marilyn and Me

Constable Dilip Mistry, the last obstacle between me and my US green card, sits at his desk, opposite me, in the hot, humid Mumbai police station, thumbing through a pile of dossiers. I sit on a hard teak chair with an upright back – a relic from the days of the Raj.

I stare at the pressed shirt buttoned right up to his Adam's apple. His starched collar digs into the skin on his neck as if it's a chain on a Rottweiler. The buttons of his shirt stretch tight across his belly. Bushy eyebrows hover over deep-set eyes.

Squashed in between the ornately carved elephant-head arms of a high-backed chair, he removes his thick glasses, rubs the bridge of his nose, and returns the heavy black frames to their paper-pushing perch. He opens and closes his right fist a few times as if he's a boxer about to launch the final punch, twists the ends of his moustache and picks up his fountain pen.

I'm invisible. He gives no sign I'm here.

A large colour portrait of Andy Warhol's Marilyn Monroe hangs on the wall behind the constable. She patiently witnesses the slow grind of bureaucracy from under blue-lidded eyes, parted scarlet lips and golden locks that match the yellow stripes on his epaulets. My knees press uncomfortably against the front panel of the narrow, beige Formica desk. Facing me, a black plastic name-tag with bold white letters proudly announces CONSTABLE DILIP MISTRY.

For my US green card application, I'm required to present a 'testimony' from the Indian police declaring that I have no criminal record in India. Raj, my company's head of administration, gets me an appointment with this police constable, who will, hopefully, process my request.

I shift in my chair. I'm squeezed in between two of my male work colleagues, who have come to help me find my way through a minefield of red tape. Raj, immobile on my right, finally lets out a long sigh and slumps. Every few minutes, Amit, his assistant, on my left, mops his forehead with his sleeve.

I stare up at Marilyn, imagining how many similar scenes she's watched. We've been sitting in this room for over an hour, and I wonder how much longer this saga will take. Marilyn's sensual smile doesn't help the constable's mood. He remains surly and inattentive as he works his way through a stack of cardboard folders. He picks one up, blows off the dust, opens it and grunts.

My nose tickles and I sneeze again and again, apologising each time. No one blinks.

A large ceiling fan creates a soft breeze. Its flaying arms slice through the thick air, filling the room with a baritone, bureaucratic buzz. The desk shakes as the constable thumps his hand on a black buzzer as if he's a judge banging the hammer in a courtroom. I jump too. The constable's desk trembles against my shins and the floor vibrates under the soles of my thin flip-flops. Trying not to smile, I purse my lips. The buzzer muffles the sound of his fountain pen nib scratching across the bottom of the sheet of paper.

The office door bursts open. A young man, in a crisp white shirt and shiny black trousers, bows his head as if he's paying homage to a god. Hair neatly combed and greased, the parting down the middle, he picks up the pile of papers thrust across the table towards him. He stands still for a moment, legs locked together, spine straight. His boss doesn't say anything. Doesn't look up. Not to him, not to me, not to my two companions. I expect the clerk to salute, but he spins around and strides out of the room. His shirt sticks to his clammy back.

In the large hall outside, index fingers click-clack on IBM golf-ball typewriters. Twenty men in white shirts and black trousers sit in three long rows on wooden benches ploughing through mounds of papers. I'm living history in the present. The silence, the particles of dust floating in the bright light, the cobwebs hanging from the high gothic ceilings. I expect to see Ronald Merrick, the grouchy British police superintendent from *Jewel of the Crown*, tapping his cane on one of the desks to 'chivvy along' the work.

The black-and-yellow epaulet on the police constable's left shoulder sways as he picks up another report. He shakes his fountain pen, signs on a dotted line and rolls a piece of blotting paper over the wet ink. He closes the folder and smacks the buzzer again with the palm of his hand. Again, the door flies open, and again the constable pushes the closed binder towards the clerk. The same scenario happens again and again. After a while, the young clerk's hair hangs limp. He bows even lower. A frown burrows into his forehead. I feel his awkwardness and sense his humiliation.

I press my palm against my forehead to calm me. Are we too going to be intimidated by this thickset man? What will I do if he becomes uncooperative? I'm due to leave India in a few months. With no US visa, I'll have to go back to London again and my move to the US will be further delayed.

A whiff of sweat and soap churned by the fan engulfs the room. Trying not to turn my head, I slip Amit a discreet glance. He mops his brow, shakes his head and looks away. We have to wait until the constable is ready. I stare out the window into the wall of a neighbouring building. The white wall streaked black from heat, humidity, mould and pollution glares back.

From underneath my shoulder-length curly hair, rivulets of sweat trickle over my shoulder blades, running down my back. I stare up at Marilyn.

Finally, Constable Mistry turns to focus on the pages of forms I've completed over the last few days. My personal biographical details and the multiple visa stamps in my passport. A paper clip attaches a strip of ten passport photos. The Indian government and other institutions must by now have over seventy photos of me. Photos for visas, photos for filing tax forms, photos to open a bank account and another for a credit card. Photos at the medical clinic, for the tenancy agreement for my flat, and for my mobile phone contract.

'Madam.' Mistry frowns at me. Wet patches appear under his armpits. 'For what you are wanting fingerprints and criminal clearance?' He rocks back on his broad chair, stroking the elephant heads on the carved arms. 'You can see I am much busy.'

Caught off balance, I try to answer but my mouth is dry. I'm daydreaming of falling in love with the handsome Charles

Dance, as Guy Perron, in *The Jewel in the Crown*. Amit coughs and nudges me with his elbow. I leave my daydream.

'Please, sir,' I reply, flicking my hair behind my ears quite deliberately. Perhaps he goes for sensuous women? *I have to try something. Maybe I can try to be more like Marilyn?* 'You see I'm applying for my US green card. At the consulate, they want your assurance that I have no criminal record here in India. I have to do the same for all the other countries I've lived in – South Africa, Israel and the UK. I would be most grateful if you could provide me with the necessary documentation.'

Staring up at Marilyn, I'm envious of her golden hair, bewitching eyes, long lashes and beguiling smile, as if she's enjoying the scene playing out below. I can almost hear her singing 'I wanna be loved by you, just you, and nobody else but you…' It makes no sense – a grumpy officer and a movie star. I beg her to help me.

Mistry grimaces and shakes his head. A delaying tactic, but Amit knows exactly when, and how, and how much. He takes an envelope out of his pocket and hands it to Constable Mistry who, without looking at it, pulls open his desk drawer and slips it in as if nothing has happened. All the while, he keeps staring at me.

I lower my gaze and try to make my eyelids heavy, sexy – just like Marilyn's.

But Mistry, obviously unimpressed, pushes his chair away from the desk. The wood scrapes against the marble floor like chalk shrieking down a blackboard. I shiver. He runs his forefinger down the forms again. The furrows in his forehead deepen.

My back is soaked. My palms clammy.

It's taken almost two years to get all the information I need for the US embassy. Months for a South African birth certificate, photos of my daughter and me together over the past twenty years to prove I'm a bona fide relative, marriage certificates, John's death certificate and X-rays to prove I don't have TB. There's always something else they want, always more hurdles to overcome. And now another delay is in the offing.

Mistry looks at Amit. 'More photos I'm needing. And a bigger size. These are small, small, small. Too small.' He grunts. 'More another ten…then maybe I'm finding one of the girls is not so much busy.' He turns to face me. 'Next week you coming back. Now time for my lunch.'

I know that lunch time is holy. A time where everyone – managers, doctors, secretaries, cleaners and drivers – are entitled to an hour's peace, even if it's only to eat a banana, a bowl of rice, vegetable samosa or *vada pao* (a potato burger, eaten on the pavement).

If Mistry goes to lunch, I'll have wasted a whole day. My interview for my green card will have to be delayed. My visa for the US may be months and months away. The thought of further chaos in my life makes me queasy. My London home rented out, my furniture in storage, where will I stay and what will I do?

Just when I've imagined that my life is beginning to feel more organised, it's beginning to fall apart again. So many things are beyond my control. Here I'm in the hands of a constable who obviously has no time for an expat's nonsense. I see his disdain for me and my colleagues. The way he strokes his whiskers and towers over me. I imagine the conversation in his head, and almost hear him say it aloud. 'Who did they think they were, anyway? Those Britishers made enough of a mess oppressing my country for almost one hundred years.'

Although I'm not British by birth, I'm still sensitive to how my colleagues and team might view me. After all, white South Africa where I'd grown up, with its cruel, oppressive apartheid system, was worse. In that stuffy room, I panic and turn to John. What would he do? But that doesn't help. I have to learn to find my own way.

I'm not quite sure where I find the gumption, the chutzpah.

'Sir, please.' I gasp. 'Maybe I get you a very big photo of me, then you can hang my photo next to Marilyn. Maybe one with a ukulele?' I stand up and shimmy my hips.

Raj pushes his hand on my shoulder, urging me to sit down. Amit goes pale.

After two hours of sitting in front of this policeman, my stomach growls and I'm thirsty. Being patient hasn't worked. Being submissive and polite hasn't worked. Baksheesh hasn't worked. Trying to be sexy hasn't worked. Maybe a joke will. What do I have to lose?

Mistry slams his fist on the table. I freeze. I've blown it. He probably feels I've mocked him. So much so, that we might have to travel to another city to get the necessary testimony. I swallow loudly as if a pill is stuck in my throat. Surely everyone hears it.

Then Mistry laughs. A deep bellow. A roar. All the way up from his belly to his mouth. I sit, stunned. I can only imagine what my two colleagues think. Pushing Amit out of the way, the cop kicks the bench over and hugs me. He takes my arm and kicks up a couple of Charleston dance steps. Mistry slaps me on the back, wipes his face with his cuff, and opens his office door. His eyes sparkle.

'Anu!'

An echo down the cavernous hall. Typewriter balls stop spinning. Rows of men jump to attention. Stiletto heels clack on the marble floor. Silver bangles jangle. A woman with jet-black hair clipped to one side rushes towards us. Her crimson sari with blue edging floats behind her.

'You're taking this foreigner lady and doing her fingerprints now. First, before you have your lunch. We are not doing any delay.'

'Of course, *suh*,' Anu mumbles, lowering her eyes. 'Right now, *suh*.'

Silence. No one moves. Only the incessant street concerto gives any indication that we're in a bustling police station in the midst of a cacophonous city. Amit mops his brow again and Raj lets out another deep sigh.

'*Shukryia*, thank you so much, sir.' I hold out my hand.

Mistry shakes it up and down a bit too vigorously, releases his grip to twirl his moustache and strides away.

I glance back at Marilyn and wink. If she were here in person, I'd hug her.

CHAPTER 17

Firewalker

'I'm unhappy with the performance of the retail business.' The chairman sits forward in his chair as he addresses the leadership meeting. 'The operating profit is eighteen point four-seven per cent below budget.'

He glares at retail's CEO. 'Baljit, your team is not working together, your efforts are not coordinated.' He raises his voice and loosens his brown paisley tie. 'You're all flying around looking busy, as if you were a swarm of blue-arsed flies hovering over a dung heap. I think you're all messing about and not addressing the key issues. Do something about it. And *quick*.'

Baljit rolls his head left to right and rubs his knuckles into his temples.

If there's no improvement in performance within the next six months, I'm going to sell off the business.' The chairman slams his fist on his engraved teak desk, staring at Baljit as a judge pronouncing sentence might. 'Hundreds of people will lose their jobs!'

No one moves. No one coughs, stirs or looks around. The air-conditioner grumbles as if shifting gears. The chairman stands up, his velvet-backed chair scraping the marble floor, and he strides, footsteps echoing, out of the boardroom, slamming the door behind him. The marble floor trembles.

When I swallow, the noise seems to echo around the room. Sitting behind Baljit, I watch the perspiration trickle down his balding head and the back of his neck, soaking his shirt collar. Blackberries buzz and team members mumble softly, cupping their mouths in the palms of their hands. 'Call you back later.'

Baljit turns to look at me. 'Susan, please, I know you must be very busy organising your next move,' he says, his voice cracking, 'but I believe you are the only one here who can help us to begin to work as a team. Our egos are so big they can't squeeze through the doors anymore. We have to learn to work together. Right now we're stuck in our silos, and no one's keen to change.'

He puts his head in his hands and lets out a long sigh. When he straightens up, I notice his red-rimmed eyes. He's been trying to sort things out, but the chairman's right. The team members bumble around in their own special areas. The finance and operations teams blame each other for the low profit margins and squabble over expenditure. I'm not sure if they all understand the business model, or even the operational jargon and acronyms we all use.

I clear my throat and look at him more closely. 'Well, if we could get the procurement team to collaborate with marketing to review the savings on bulk buying – that would be up to twenty per cent…' I pause, watching his face begin to lighten. 'That would be a good start.' I take a sip of cold chai, not caring that there's a milky film on it.

Baljit's eyes suddenly widen. 'And if the operations team worked with the customer service associates, more customers would come into the store, and spend more.' He stretches his arms up to the ceiling.

'Let me map out an agenda for a two-day workshop and we can discuss it tomorrow.' Wiping my mouth with a paper napkin, I stand up and pull my sticky kameez off the back of my legs.

'Thank you, thank you, thank you so much.'

'See you tomorrow.' As I turn to walk out the door, one sandal slips off my foot and I stop to slide it back on. That's when I notice the team has already left.

Baljit shouts after me. 'Hey, Susan, wait. I just got a great idea.' He rubs the palms of his hands together. I stop and turn to face him. 'There's this guy, who used to be an officer in the army, and is now working as a team builder, trainer. I hear he has a couple of outdoor exercises that we can add to the end of the agenda each day.' Baljit's Blackberry buzzes but he ignores it. 'This guy will for sure build our confidence. He will make us all stand tall and proud, and he will give us that "can do" attitude. You need do nothing. Leave it to me. Please make sure we have two hours at the end of each day for him.'

I nod.

Baljit picks up his notepad, clips a ballpoint onto his shirt pocket, and touches my shoulder as we walk out of the room together without another word.

Later that evening, Baljit calls, saying he has spoken with Santosh. He suggests introducing an unorthodox agenda item – walking across shards of glass and burning coals.

'Not a good idea, Baljit.' I balk as if I'm a horse refusing to jump over a hurdle. 'Those activities may be good for young guys in the army. But you're a bunch of guys in their forties and fifties. And what about Shalini? How's she going to feel about this?' I turn down the volume on the TV news. 'There've been lawsuits after people loaded with hash or alcohol burned their feet on glowing coals. Some people are so traumatised and humiliated in front of their colleagues and bosses, they resign.' I pace up and down the living room as we speak, still staring at the TV. 'My God,' I say, not caring that I'm interrupting our conversation, 'did you see that seventeen Indian soldiers were killed in an avalanche in Kashmir?'

Baljit breathes into his phone. 'So many tragedies in this country every day, Susan. Kashmir is always a problem. What to do.' He yells at his kids to keep quiet before returning his attention to me. 'Just listen to what Santosh has to say, please. If you still think it's a bad idea, we'll drop it.'

I call Santosh right then and meet him at a nearby café for lunch the next day.

'These people must be learning about the power of attitude,' Santosh says, fanning his mouth. The chilli is strong even for him. 'Otherwise, how could they possibly implement the strategic plan that you will be helping them at the offsite?' I sip my chilled lassi to cool my tongue, unable to answer. 'The challenges of these exercises, ma'am, will, I'm promising you, help them be courageous, and overcome all the potential obstacles they think are in their way.'

My eyes water. I sniff and suck in some cool air.

'The managers are having to learn about their own inner strength,' Santosh adds, crossing one foot over his knee. He leans over the table and continues, 'You must be trusting me. They are needing to learn to work together as a team and support each other. You will see. You, too, will do it.'

My eyes water and my mouth burns from the spicy chilli. Sniffling, I can only mumble, 'Okay,' pausing before adding, 'but *I'm* not doing it.'

I rifle through my tote for a tissue to blow my nose. Santosh looks down at the table. There's too much ahead at stake for me, and too much to do – handing over to my successor, packing up the flat, coordinating with the mover, and attending a number of farewell parties. I won't be able to do all that with festering feet and swollen legs. I make that quite clear again – to Santosh and later to the management team. I won't be an active participant in the outdoor activities.

'You're right,' Baljit accedes. 'We don't want you to leave sick.'

He doesn't know that my impending move to the US has already made me sick. Another new start in another new land where I'll have to look for another new job, move into a new home, buy new appliances, and sort out the endless bureaucracy to get healthcare, a driver's license, a bank account and credit card, and set up Wi-Fi. Not to mention buying a new laptop, phone and printer. *And* filing tax returns in three countries. Most mornings I'm jarred awake before sunrise, feeling as fragile as a porcelain doll. *Touch me and I'll crack.* I stare up at the revolving ceiling fan, hoping it will solve all my problems.

The first evening of our workshop begins with a challenge. In an open field outside the training centre Santosh rolls out a twenty-foot-long tarpaulin covered with broken bottles. We cheer, clap and whistle, as each executive staggers barefoot across the smashed glass, swaying as if they're walking on a swinging footbridge. I bite my bottom lip and mumble silent prayers to myself. No one stumbles. No one falls. Santosh sits each participant down on a stool after the first rite of passage and, tweezers in hand, checks the soles of each foot for glass splinters.

'It's nothing, Susan,' they tell me as they stand. 'It doesn't hurt at all. You must be doing it.'

If they can do it...

I rise. I hesitate. I question my sanity as I stand on the edge of the path, staring at the chunks of glass winking back at me. The jaws of a great white shark look up. I don't think about what I'm doing, or why. No great epiphany comes to mind. Not confident enough to go alone, I ask for help. As Baljit holds onto my left arm and Santosh my right, I begin the journey across that river of shattered bottles, wobbling as if I'm a gymnast tottering on the balance beam. Supported not only by my two handlers, but also by the cheering and clapping of the team, I move forward.

A fakir on a bed of nails, I expect blood to fountain from my feet. I take forever to traverse the flat surface before I tumble into Santosh's waiting arms hollering as if I'm a cowgirl lassoing a bronco.

Slapping me on the back, he takes hold of my elbow as I sit down on a three-legged plastic stool. I feel tingling but no pain. *None.* Santosh tweezes a few splinters from the soles of my feet. I can't stop smiling. That journey across those shards of glass begins to lift the heavy load of loss that I have been hauling around. The sadness is still locked inside, but the burden is lighter. I will sleep well tonight, I imagine. And I do.

On the second day of the exercises, the team and I work on the business plan in a room surrounded by flip charts, PowerPoint presentations, financial projections and a training programme for new store managers. There's a renewed energy in the room as if everyone is betting on a winning racehorse. Customer checkout time will be faster, spoilage reduced, and shelves fully stocked. Debates are spirited, people bickering, agreeing, raising their voices and in the end committing to a plan of action. No one pays much attention to the endless texts and phone calls that are so typical in our business culture. The challenging 'glass' exercise begins to build their confidence. And mine too.

That evening I expect some of the team to resist the fire-walking exercise. It's a crazy stunt at best, especially after all the productive work the team did that day.

But I'm wrong again.

The white-hot coals are spread out a few inches thick on a flat sandy stretch near Mumbai's Juhu beach. The radiating heat, which I can feel five or six metres away, deters no one.

All twelve members of the retail leadership team who have already completed the run – some more than once – form a wide circle around the embers to coax me on. Hands slap against bongo drums, tambourines jingle, and a trumpet blares an unfamiliar tune. I imagine slipping and falling and going up in flames. I see John's coffin sliding into the flaming maw at the crematorium, and me flying in after him! Sati. On John's funeral pyre, like the thousands of women before me.

'C'mon, Susan, you can do it too,' Santosh says, but I shake my head. 'No way.'

The night air is thick with smoke. Through my smog-streaked glasses, everything is a blur.

And yet I'm hypnotised by the glowing coals, seduced by the rhythmic maracas shakers and whistling colleagues and spurred on by my ego. My legs, independent limbs, walk towards the edge of the fire. Disembodied. Doped. Disobedient. A helicopter *chop-chop-chops* overhead. A mosquito lands on my cheek and I slap it, my palm slimy with its blood.

I've nothing left to prove. I proved all last night when I hobbled over twenty metres of glass shards. This further madness makes no sense.

Still, all I think about is this: I may never have the chance to walk on fire again. Not *ever*.

Eucalyptus resin from the charred logs wafts around me as I hike my cotton shalwar up to my knees, close my eyes, and breathe long and deep. Under the trees a couple of crows bicker over a half-eaten samosa in a tug of war. In time to the birds' pulling and shifting, I take a step back on my right foot and onto my left and rock back again.

'Go, Susan, go!' The crowd eggs me on in unison.

John, his breath warm and smelling of fresh mint, whispers, '*Go.*'

I can't let him down.

The trumpeting reaches a crescendo, the drumming is faster, frenzied, as I sprint across the inferno. Elbows flapping, I count each step out loud. 'One, two, three…sixteen, seventeen…'

The soles of my feet touch cool sand. My kameez doesn't catch fire, nor does my skin blister. There's no smell of singed hair. I can't seem to recall the heat under my feet. But I do remember the team's whistling, clapping and the high-pitched trumpeting. And I recall feeling stronger and more confident than ever before – and ready for my next move.

Panting and laughing, I raise my arms into the air and join in the ululating chorus. I drop onto a wooden stool a few yards away from the fire, nearly tipping over.

'Put your feet into this tub of cold water,' Santosh says.

Perspiration rolls off my scalp and my hair sticks to the back of my neck. Someone gives me a can of Kingfisher beer. I pull the tab and gulp down the icy brew. Santosh daubs and massages aloe vera gel on the soles of my feet, now beginning to sting lightly, as if he's stroking a baby's cheeks.

Slipping on my flip-flops, I stand up on shaky legs, expecting to feel some pain. Even though I don't feel any discomfort, I shuffle towards the rest of the team as though my soles are blistered. They should be.

Raising my beer can, I make a toast. 'Now that we've survived wobbling barefoot across shards of glass and walking across fire, let's ask ourselves what else are we capable of doing?'

'To the bottom line,' the team cheers. 'We can do it. To the bottom line! We can do *anything*!'

I feel the sudden swell of pride welling within me. 'As you all know, I'm leaving India in two days, so I was determined not to participate in these last two exercises.' I press the cold beer can against my forehead. 'Like many of you who were anxious about participating in them, I was scared. I imagined boarding my flight in a wheelchair with bandaged, bleeding and blistered feet.'

A spark flies up in the air. My eyes follow it. Life is as fleeting as that.

'But this morning, when I saw how you finally began to face your problems head-on with our current business model, I realised that I too feel stronger and readier to face my new life in a new land.'

A plane flies low, drowning out any further conversation. 'Khudaya Ve – Luck', the latest Bollywood hit, blares out over the loudspeakers. Feet shuffle in time to the rhythm, hips sway, and the team sings along. The workshop is officially over, and it's time to relax.

I tilt my head back to get the last drops of beer and realise that over the past few months I've obsessed less about John's illness and death and remember more of the great times we had together. Grief is finally on a journey, shifting out of my frontal lobe and travelling into the spare room of my mind. There's a new sense of meaning to my life. Even Mumbai's urban pollution, a yellowish glow hanging in the night sky, can't stop my future stretching out before me towards a distant horizon.

I no longer feel the need to prove how strong I am. I realise at last that, even without John, that feeling of being as useless as a discarded condom is gone. I can still talk to him, ask his opinions, and enjoy his favourite meals without him.

Baljit touches me on my shoulder and takes hold of my forearm to escort me to the buffet, more like a banquet dinner, laid out on white tablecloths over trestle tables. Silver buffet dishes overflow with creamy dal, naan bread, roasted masala cauliflower, and potatoes roasted with garlic. Oil lamps flicker, chasing away the shadows.

I wish I could bottle up every one of the haunting fragrances; fenugreek, cumin, curry leaves, cinnamon and green mango chutney into a memory closet and open each at will.

This is my last engagement with this team, and I find myself wishing I could stay longer. But this is no longer practical. My contract and work visa expire in a week, and my next Seattle grandchild is due to enter our world any day now. As I walk away from the music, laughter and chatter, I feel John stroking my shoulders and holding my cheeks in his broad hands. His lips touch mine. John walked through death. And when he died, I walked through death too.

Now I can keep walking through this fire – and whatever other fires lie ahead. Otherwise, a little part of me will continue to die each day, and I promised John I'd live on for us both.

CHAPTER 18

The Cricket Cure

It's my last week at work, and my co-workers can talk of nothing else except my farewell party. But they're not concerned about the menu as much as they are about the highlight of the day: the cricket match before the banquet. Everyone has something to say about it – the gardeners, dishwashers, receptionists, cleaners, trainers and executives.

I'm the star player. Bets are laid on how many runs I'll make. The final arbiter is the office video camera, all charged and ready to go.

I crowed about how at elementary school I played the dangerous position of wicket keeper catching the ball, smacking the stumps and getting the batsman out. I flaunted the fact that I often scored more than fifty runs in an innings, and teased that I could take them for a 'six', right over the boundary and would show them how far I could crack that ball. So they took me seriously, determined to give me a chance to show my worth.

Although I'd normally be a bit apprehensive about living up to my reputation, after walking on broken glass and fire, nothing fazes me anymore. I'm up for any challenge.

In India, cricket is a national obsession. On the days of international cricket matches, kids skip school with their parents' blessings, and adults stay home from work – or if they do go, they do very little. Waiters ignore customers, policemen disregard pickpockets and villains, and gangsters come above ground. Everyone is a cricket junkie: bankers, waiters, teachers, nannies, doctors, street cleaners and tea *wallahs*. If they're not watching the game on TV, they're constantly checking the score on their mobiles.

Sachin, the star batsman for the Indian cricket team, is a celebrity. On our executive floor, shouts of '*Sachin kitne pe khada hai*' – 'Sachin is not out! How much has he scored?' – echo down corporate corridors and reverberate across meeting rooms.

Soon after I arrived in Mumbai we drove past a sandy cricket 'pitch' – an area the size of a bus littered with peanut shells, corn husks and coconut husks, and squeezed in between rows of corrugated iron shacks in a narrow lane known as a gally, near a public latrine. Emaciated dogs nosed around rotten potato peels lying at the side of the road. A few yards away, women lined up in floral polyester saris at the only visible faucet. They sidled away with plastic pots on their heads, hips swaying, anklets tinkling.

Back in England, cricket games are held on huge expanses of immaculate green lawns at schools, parks and village greens. At Lord's Cricket Ground in London, the only bats allowed on the pitch are paddle-shaped and exactly four-and-a-quarter inches wide and thirty-eight inches long. Willow trees cultivated for the sole purpose of making these bats are shaped and sanded by master cricket bat-makers. Quality is rated on the straightness of the grain and bats can cost up to six hundred pounds. Deep-crimson cricket balls are made from a cork core, layered with tightly wound string and covered by a leather case with a raised, sewn seam – slightly smaller, lighter and firmer than a baseball.

At British clubs and village greens, cricket games and matches are dignified affairs. No shouting from team members, and no spectators screaming instructions at the players. Tea with watercress-and-cucumber sandwiches with no crusts are served promptly at 4 p.m. They're accompanied by clotted cream scones, fruitcake and shortbread. Players wear cream trousers, ivory shirts, white V-necked pullovers, spiked white cricket shoes and cream leg guards. They are obliged by tradition to behave like gentlemen and 'go light' on the beer.

Driving past the slum near my Mumbai home during those early days, I stared through my car window at a ragtag cricket match. The players, their feet bare, their hair matted, and their shorts and shirts either one size too big or too small, leaned forward, focused and ready to play.

One boy, the batsman, held a bat made from a bent, discarded metal pole. Another, the bowler, lobbed the ball – made of rags wrapped in plastic bags and tied up with string – towards the batsman. *Thwack*! The bundle landed on the bonnet of our car amid cheers of, 'Six, a six, *merrim*! So sorry, *merrim*, but he is our Sachin.'

Skinny arms waved and high-fives exploded. The boys played cricket in that squalid alley as if they'd been popping champagne corks in a large field of freshly mown lawn, ringed by oak trees and grandstands.

Their excitement was contagious. I asked Khamat to pull

over, and I got out of the car and reached out to shake the boys' hands, gently slapping scrawny backs through stained T-shirts. Then I paid the vendor of a nearby cart to give them each a popsicle.

Khamat raised his voice. '*Merrim*, you must be careful here. Those boys are very much naughty.' He frowned. 'Too much hanky-panky.'

He was probably right. We'd be mobbed next time we drove by, but I didn't care. It was a small turning point for me. I was slowly climbing down from the grandstand and beginning to take a swing at life again.

But it's not my auspicious beginnings with cricket in India that emboldens my team to plan a cricket match for my last afternoon in Mumbai. I've been foolish enough to brag that, growing up in South Africa, I know all about cricket. That as a child my dad and I watched many five-day, international cricket matches at the Wanderers Club in Johannesburg. We picnicked on the lawn as he taught me all I needed to know. As we munched on cheese-and-tomato sandwiches and sipped tea with sweetened condensed milk from a Thermos, Dad described how the bowler is supported by nine fielders and a wicket keeper. Their job is to catch or stop the ball. I understood that it's important for the batsman to hit it far enough away from the fielders to allow himself to run to the other end of the pitch before the ball could be returned to the wicket keeper. He also taught me how to hold a bat and bowl a spinner.

On the day of our own company match, which is being held in the street leading to the imposing marble entrance of the corporate offices – a wide sandy lane that's filled with potholes and gravel and lined with small shops. No expats or 'foreigners' live or work in the neighbourhood.

The cricket pitch is marked with chalk and the 'field' extends to a tyre repair shanty, a barber's wooden-box chair with a mirror hanging on a pole, and a butcher's, where chickens cluck their hearts out in wooden cages and a bleating goat stands tethered to a street pole.

We gather in the middle of the road as two team captains – a cook and the finance manager – choose their teams. The umpires, a dishwasher and trainer, blow their whistles. Families lean over the railings of their balconies, welders turn off their blowtorches, carpenters cease hammering and sawing, shopkeepers fold their arms and tell customers to come back later, cyclists get off their bikes and pedestrians stand frozen.

I'm the first to bowl. Raising my arms and clapping, I'm confident I can put on a good show. But I soon learn that everyone – cooks, cleaners and managers – are as good as British top-tier club level players. They've been playing cricket since they could walk, whenever they get a chance, with whatever they can use for bat and ball, and wherever they can find a small patch of ground.

The batsman, twenty yards away from me at the other end of the pitch, bends over, points the flat side of his bat towards me and nods. Hopefully, he'll miss the ball and it will crack into the wickets behind him, or the wicket keeper will catch the ball as it bounces off his bat.

The street is quiet as I spit on the ball and wipe it on my thigh like a pro, and sprint towards the bowling crease. My arm whirls over my head like the blades of a fan. Vermillion drop earrings wobble at my earlobes like a turkey's snood.

Gold sandals glint in the afternoon sunlight. Thankfully the ball flies straight down the pitch and not into the spectators. The batsman cracks the ball for a six – way over the boundary without ever touching the ground.

'She's a *dibbly dobbly*!' yells the butcher from across the road.

He's right. The balls that I bowl are too slow and too easy to hit. I high-five my team captain who politely puts me out to field. The stakes are too high for me to bowl another over.

My replacement bowler hits the bails twice and the level of the game improves. The opposition is out. With our team up, it's my turn to bat. I stare, trying to stay in control as our security guard, the bowler, lowers his head and charges towards me as if he's a bull about to gore a matador. I want to run off the pitch. The ball flies down the narrow pitch with the speed of a racing car.

'Careful, *merrim*,' Giresh the gardener shouts. 'That's a googly – he's always making it spin very, very much.'

The ball spins all right, and turns towards my front leg as I jump aside, hoping not to be knocked flat on my back. With a will all its own, the ball hits the bat with a loud crack. My arms feel as if they're about to be pulled out of their sockets. I whack the ball, as if I'm Sachin hitting a six. One run. Onlookers whistle, clap and cheer. Phones snap photos and the video camera buzzes. I lift my bat in a victory sign.

I miss the next ball as it belts towards me and smashes into the wicket. Amid hissing and catcalls, the stumps collapse like a felled cedar tree. I punch a defiant fist in the air. My cheeks hurt from laughing. Even the bowler raises his arms and claps.

A rumble and incessant honking interrupt the cheering. A

truck moves towards us. Without thinking, I sprint towards it and, brandishing my arms, yell at the driver, '*Idhar ruko!*' Stop.

Dust churns around my feet. Someone tugs the sleeve of my ultramarine kurta, trying to pull me off the road. I know that vehicles brake for no one. Not for cripples hopping on one leg, nor for old women barely able to shuffle and young men straining to heave carts overladen with watermelons.

Where is this crazy bravado coming from? What am I doing?

The crowds shift to the side, but I dash defiantly towards the driver, holding up my palms, signalling once again for him to stop. His eyes shut tight and then open again, bulging like a bullfrog. He stares straight at me as if I'm an alien from space. The last thing he expects to see is a middle-aged white woman telling him to halt. I must have looked like an ethereal being in a cloak of dust. Barely visible. But just enough movement and colour to cause the honking to subside and his brakes to shriek. I wave away the clouds of grit and walk up to the driver's cabin.

'*Shukriya*, thank you.' I smile and bow towards him, my hands respectfully pressed together at the front of my chest. I step up onto the running board next to the driver and extend my hand in gratitude. Then I move my index finger in a circle, hoping he understands that he should back up and make a detour.

Sign language worked before and it works now. Too shaken to do anything else, he shifts the truck into reverse and backs up to the corner. Rhythmic clapping erupts from the bystanders.

I strut back to our cricket pitch yelling, 'Yay, okay!' and the game goes on.

At that moment, I feel John looking down and seeing me there coated in dust and perspiration and revelling in my bravery. I remember my jovial, romantic and robust husband, rather than a ravaged, sunken and sweaty asbestos victim. I hear his voice calling me his bobby dazzler for the first time in ages.

For three and a half years, I've learned to live my life completely differently than before – with an appreciation of beauty in the most unexpected places. I've been humbled at Varanasi, learned to breathe deep and meditate at my yoga, and overcome my fears during the massacre.

Crimson sunrises and aromas of garlic, celery and papayas in my local market roused me to want to take one deep breath after another. At first, I couldn't quite understand what was happening. That glow that flowed through me when I attended five-day wedding extravaganzas, danced in the streets on the birthday of Ganesh, the elephant god and wore a red Santa hat with a white pompom at Christmas.

Staring at the crowd around us on that dusty Mumbai 'cricket pitch', tears trickle down my cheeks. I'm deeply moved that everyone has gone to so much trouble to organise the event.

In the end, my team loses. The staff gloats. Nothing like beating the boss's team.

Plum and aquamarine valances decorate the farewell banquet on the office rooftop. Magenta tassels adorn the pinnacles. Silver chafing dishes filled with fresh spinach and paneer, creamy chickpea curry with saffron rice sit on a large round table. I sip chilled coconut milk straight out of the fuzzy husk through a straw and nibble on a vegetable samosa.

Someone throws a garland of pungent marigolds over my

head. A fragrance that follows me from the first time I smelled those garlands on the barge when John and I first came to India together. Marigolds that followed me from Kerala to Varanasi, and finally now on my last evening in Mumbai. An intense aroma that I can almost taste and breathe, reminding me of the twelve blissful years that John and I enjoyed together.,

Bollywood strains of *'Dil toh bachcha hai jee'* – 'My heart is like a naïve child', blast through the loudspeakers. Men whistle and gyrate their hips. Women ululate and pull me into the middle of a whirlpool of arms, vermillion lipstick and jangling bangles. I spin in a circle as if performing a whirling dervish. When I finally stop, bent over laughing and gasping all at once, the floor doesn't tilt and I don't feel dizzy.

By the time we finish partying, it's midnight and time for me to leave for the airport.

Where else will I ever have such fun again? Feel so brave again? There's been no time for routine or familiarity. Each day has had a different feel and smell about it: a power failure during the chairman's PowerPoint presentation to shareholders; an elephant loping along on the side of a road; a Bollywood wedding party spilling out onto the streets.

I know Seattle is going to be quiet in comparison, but now I can't wait to live near my own family and play with my grandchildren. Filled with the energy and excitement of a team decades younger, I'm ready. I've grown stronger, more independent and learned to be so much more grateful for who I am and what I have.

This afternoon I stood in front of the wicket, cricket bat in hand, and walloped the attacking ball despite my shaking fingers. I held onto that bat even as my toes, thighs and back wobbled under its force. Is it possible that I ran straight towards a truck thundering down the dusty street as it flew past the potholes? Did it really screech to a halt because of me?

Who could have guessed that cricket would become a symbol of beginnings and endings for me in India? My farewell party will always remind me of how brave I can be. How I've come to understand that I can cope and adapt to new and often desperate situations. That I'm stronger than I ever realised.

I travelled to India as a grieving widow. *A mullygrubbe* – a cricket ball that doesn't bounce after pitching. Three and a half years later and I'm leaving as *a biffer* – a big hitter. As I pack my trinkets, kitschy jewellery and embroidered kurtas, I realise that I'm no washout. My game is far from over. I felt ready for the cricket match and banquet just as much as I do now for my move to the US to live near my family.

On my last sultry Indian evening, I whirled and twirled Bollywood style – shimmying hips, flowing long hair and playful bracelets. I filled my heart with aromas of cardamom and fenugreek. The raw, fragrant, distinctly acrid marigolds floating around my shoulders and neck, were an aura of life. I'm sad that my time in India came to an end, but I look out at a new chapter in my life.

As I stare up into the magenta sky, Venus, a later riser, comes to life. First a pale yellow, then a more intense, resplendent, canary yellow, magnetic, irresistible.

What an incredible ride I've had.

CHAPTER 19

Through the Rabbit Hole

Someone is speaking Hindi and then English, but the words make no sense. My head feels hungover-heavy. I try to remember where I am. The details settle into place like a dream, an image, becoming both more visible and invisible all at the same time. An involuntary snort escapes up my nose and I turn my head from right to left to see if anyone heard me. That embarrassing snore that comes from nowhere whenever I doze off on a plane.

My eye mask slips up onto my forehead.

When I shift my body upright, my right leg cramps. I jiggle it and the burning sensation eases. I must have settled into an awkward position during that long journey from Mumbai, but still my foot doesn't move. My ankle is stuck under the seat in front of me.

I lean forward, take in a long, deep breath to try to steady myself and slowly ease my foot out. Just in time, as the flight attendant flips my seat into an upright position. My shoulders jolt forward. I want to say, *Hey, I nearly lost my foot, here!* but my tongue feels too thick and dry to speak, the lingering taste of milk chocolate on my palate.

'*Oops*, my apologies,' she says as if reading my mind. She

straightens up, and leans over to push up the window shade, leaving me in a cloud of heather-scented soap. 'These chairs have a mind of their own.'

Sunlight streams into the plane's cabin. Wing flaps turn down in preparation for landing. Engines drone louder. I twist the cap off my water bottle, tip my head back and take a gulp.

Yet again, all that's familiar – the firm mattress under a mosquito net, the soothing hum of the ceiling fan, my colleagues' chatter, the never-ending honking and mobile phone chimes, silver anklets tinkling with charms, drop earrings with blue and red stones, jade-and-orange-embroidered kurtas – is about to disappear, leaving me feeling untethered. Yet again, I walk through Alice's looking-glass, and tumble down the rabbit hole and into a new world.

I stumbled into an unfamiliar world when John was diagnosed with mesothelioma. I sank deeper when he died. I became a grief-stricken husk of a person, angry, depressed, when I moved from London to Mumbai, when I changed jobs, and sold our Islington home and all our dreams along with it. So I recognise the symptoms of dealing with the unknown and feelings of helplessness.

This time I won't surrender to fatigue or sink into a prolonged grief disorder – alone and lonely.

Panic, I've learned, is a bad counsellor.

Wisdom, my new mentor, whispers with calm control. 'Remember how you walked on burning coals and shards of glass at the leadership workshop. Remember the time when the traffic near Mumbai's international airport was gridlocked for almost half an hour, so you got out of the car with your roller bag and sprinted half a kilometre to the airport terminal facing oncoming traffic, holding up a hand to the honking drivers. And remember the *Ganga Aarti* where you said your final goodbyes to John in Varanasi?'

My head rolls from left to right and then left again.

Yes, I'm stronger now.

There's a grinding sound as landing wheels reach out for the ground. Wing flaps tilt up. The nose edges skyward and the engines howl as the plane throttles back. On this late March afternoon, we fly through a stretch of pale-blue sky filled with patchy, undulating clouds resembling translucent fish scales.

'Mackerel sky, mackerel sky, never long wet, never long dry.' I whisper the words to the ditty and stop suddenly. It's been years since I sang that to my kids. The corners of my lips turn upward.

Wisdom is a persistent guide. 'Remember how during the Mumbai massacre, your strength helped Moshe's grandparents listen to your insistent counsel and take baby Moshe's nanny, Sandra, back to Israel with them to help care for the toddler?'

I nod. *Yes. Yes.*

'Know this,' the voice in my head persists. 'When John got ill, you built up a fragile toughness to help you try to show your family and friends and colleagues that you were doing fine, even though grief sucked the softness from your heart. You've changed now.'

I think of all the times I tried to show how well I was coping. Our trips to Paris, Marrakesh and Florida, with a bag of OxyContin; brunch and lunch invitations to friends and family, and walks on Hampstead Heath. All to help John to try to live a normal life. But then the colour was sucked out of our lives. And when John died, I died too.

As the plane lurches to a halt, the seatbelt sign goes off, buckles click open, and fellow passengers stand up. A blast of cool air blows down from the ceiling vent, urging me to follow suit. I slip my eye mask into my backpack, text my daughter telling her that I've landed and take out my passport and green card to ready myself for a new phase in my life.

Standing in the slow-moving line to pass through immigration, I'm no longer in the present. I walk through each room of my recently sold London home in the Google Maps of my mind. The living room with the navy-and-white-striped sofa, where I'd sling my legs over John's to snuggle closer as we watched the nine o'clock news. The aromas of garlic, rosemary and roast lamb in the kitchen while we sipped rosé and nibbled on cashews at the granite counter. The bathroom with the huge clawfoot tub where we soaked in lavender bubble baths, washing each other's backs. And our bedroom, where we loved and laughed, and where John took his last breath, tethered to an oxygen tank, my palm on his.

The light at the booth is green, and someone shouts, 'Next.'

The immigration official takes my passport, opens it to the photo pages and stares up at my face, then down at the passport and back up at me. He picks up the rubber stamp from the counter but puts it down again. He rubs the back of his neck with one hand.

'India, *huh?*' he says. 'What were you doing there?'

I feel my shoulders hunching, swallow and try to stop biting the inside of my lip. 'I worked in a company to open a chain of supermarkets.'

He stares at me, frowns and nods. There's the sweet thump of rubber on paper.

'Welcome to the USA,' he says, and hands my passport and green card back to me.

'Thank you,' I say, my voice cracking.

My hand is shaking as I open my purse and zip these precious documents inside the pocket. I force myself to walk not run towards the escalator down to the baggage claim area.

Don't look suspicious.

A buzzer sounds and the carousal clatters into action. Blue, black and brown suitcases, each with its own story, bump past me on uneven rubber slats. Over the past four years my purple suitcases have visited India, Thailand, Egypt, the UK, the US, Israel and Johannesburg. They have many stories to tell.

Four years ago, standing at the exit to Mumbai airport at midnight, I may have looked confident in my black business suit, inappropriate nylon stockings and stiletto heels, but I felt scared. Scared of what I would do if I couldn't find my driver. Scared of being lost in an unfamiliar country and culture. Scared of never finding my way out of market alleys and scared I'd get lost looking for John. That was then. *Then* when I was someone else.

It all makes sense now.

The conveyor belt trundles on, and the narrative I've been telling myself of why I went to India after John died changes. It hadn't been about moving on. Subconsciously I hoped to rekindle the peace and joy that John and I enjoyed when we visited India four years before his diagnosis, welcoming the New Year on a barge in Kerala, laughing as we searched for Orion and Taurus. In my grieving fantasy, without understanding why, I realise I'd gone to India desperate to slide on a continuum of the life John and I shared together.

That's gone now.

I now know that my time in India gave me the opportunity to begin a new, eventful and unfamiliar journey in the shadow of my new identity as a widow. I blundered along trying to fit in by wearing kurtas and pantaloons in buttercup-yellow and scarlet, licking my fingers as I scooped dal and chana masala with chapatti. I went on long monsoon hikes to the Mahuli Fort in the hills near Mumbai, and didn't wince when a chilli burnt my tongue and turned my cheeks scarlet. When I suffered agonising stomach cramps at midnight, I woke a rickshaw driver who was asleep on a bench at the entrance to my block of flats, and was able to tell him in my Hindi to take me to the Lilivatti hospital.

At the baggage claim in Seattle's bustling airport, my suitcases wobble at the edge of the carousel. I heave them onto the floor, stand them upright, grip the handles and turn to walk to the pick-up area, where my daughter is waiting.

I couldn't have known then why I'd choose to travel to remote and harsh destinations. Camping in the bundu in a pup tent in a wildlife reserve in Namibia, where my guide confided in me that he came from a family of killers. A remote Peruvian village where I was bitten by a stray dog, taking a cargo boat to try to get to Lima before rabies got me. Completing Wainwright's strenuous coast-to-coast England hike, my boots sinking in the Yorkshire bog, as I plodded on through the sleet. Surviving the stare of a python in Tanzania when I suffer from extreme ophidiophobia – merely watching a snake on television makes me uneasy. Perhaps my parents' earliest overseas adventures inspired me to shift out of my comfort zone.

When I finally arrive at my new home and open my suitcases,

I'll find four notebooks at the bottom of one of them. The blue one, smudged with monsoon mould, is filled with notes about my tumble into widowhood. Another, smudged with tears, was written during the Mumbai massacre, tormented by toddler Moshe's pale, expressionless face. The brown Moleskin is filled with memories from Varanasi and my final farewell to John and has a dark ring from a coffee mug on the cover. The last one, filled with scribbles and comments about my farewell dinner and a cricket match, completes the set.

I walk on through an automatic door with a sign: EXIT ONLY – NO RETURN.

ACKNOWLEDGEMENTS

I began writing *Travels with my Grief* in the backseat of a car during my daily four-hour commute in Mumbai. Family and friends who held my hand during John's illness and passing joined me on my travels to explore another side of India.

Thanks to Brenda Peterson and our writing group who read first and second and third drafts; to writing coach, Amy Gigi Alexander's invaluable mentorship, to D.J. Herda, for working wonders with the final draft; and to Exprimez's Matthew Smith, whose unique insights made publication possible.

ABOUT THE AUTHOR

Susan Bloch is an award-winning author of fiction and non-fiction, as well as a leading executive coach. Bloch's essays have appeared in a variety of publications, including the *Huffington Post*, *Tikkun*, and *The Forward*. Her essays have won a prize in the *Travelers' Tales Solas Awards* and received a notable mention in *Best American Essays 2017*. She is also the author of books on leadership and board effectiveness, published in German, Brazilian Portuguese, Polish, Chinese and Turkish. A lifelong traveler, Susan lived in South Africa, New York, Tel Aviv, London, and Mumbai before alighting in Seattle. susanblochwriter.com.

twitter.com/monsue8

facebook.com/susan.bloch.58

linkedin.com/in/susan-bloch-b562278

globallearnings.com

Find out more about RedDoor
Press and sign up to our
newsletter to hear about our
latest releases, author events,
exciting **competitions**
and more at

reddoorpress.co.uk

YOU CAN ALSO FOLLOW US:

 @RedDoorBooks

 Facebook.com/RedDoorPress

 @RedDoorBooks